Diseases of Canaries

By

ROBERT STROUD

Edited by

HERBERT C. SANBORN, PH.D.
Vanderbilt University

Distributed in the U.S.A. by T.F.H. Publications, Inc., 211 West Sylvania Avenue, P.O. Box 27, Neptune City, N.J. 07753; in England by T.F.H. (Gt. Britain) Ltd., 13 Nutley Lane, Reigate, Surrey; in Canada to the book store and library trade by Clarke, Irwin & Company, Clarwin House, 791 St. Clair Avenue West, Toronto 10, Ontario; in Canada to the pet trade by Rolf C. Hagen Ltd., 3225 Sartelon Street, Montreal 382, Quebec; in Southeast Asia by Y.W. Ong, 9 Lorong 36 Geylang, Singapore 14; in Australia and the south Pacific by Pet Imports Pty. Ltd., P.O. Box 149, Brookvale 2100, N.S.W., Australia. Published by T.F.H. Publications Inc. Ltd., The British Crown Colony of Hong Kong. Printed in Hong Kong.

PREFACE

I am very glad to assist in bringing the present work to the attention of everybody interested in the pathology of birds, not merely of the canary, but also of every sort of domesticated fowl; since it seems to me that the author has done here a piece of pioneer work that is important both theoretically and practically. In many respects the performance is marvelous, when one considers the conditions under which the author acquired his preliminary knowledge of the field involved and the almost insuperable difficulties under which he performed experimentation which has upon it the genuine scientific stamp.

Several years ago, I myself began an experiment in the inheritance of song in birds (published in the "Journal of Comparative Psychology" for June and August, 1932); so that it became necessary for me to establish an aviary in which I have had since that time some three hundred to five hundred song birds, most of them foreign species, among which were a certain number of roller canaries. For a time everything went along famously, but my experience with other animals should have told me that this was not the sort of thing to be expected for either men or animals, when brought together in such an abnormally large group.

It was of course not very long before I had on my hands a first class epidemic of what I afterwards learned to be septic fever. Just how it came to be introduced into my aviary is difficult now to determine; since upon reflection I found that about all the causes mentioned by Mr. Stroud in this book were present. It was sufficient for me to find birds literally dying like flies. The amount of work done by me at the suggestion of those

PREFACE

who had remedies which they believed in was enormous; but I secured practically no results until I learned of the remedies developed by Mr. Stroud. My first attempt to use his remedy was almost as disastrous as the ravages of the disease; since I had given the medicine in metal containers and it is probable that chemical combinations were formed with these by the constituents of the specific which were highly poisonous. Nothing had been said about this eventuality in the directions given with the medicine; and I believe that my unfortunate experience first brought this aspect of the matter to Mr. Stroud's attention.

In later correspondence with him, I came to believe that I had to do with a medical man who had been carrying on experimentation as a sort of avocation; since he called my attention to certain oversights and some negligence in my methods which showed me that he had a strictly scientific attitude toward the whole situation. To say that I was amazed when I was informed that he had, without schooling, taught himself chemistry, biology, etc., so well that he had been able, under the conditions of prison life, to perform original experimentation, is expressing it mildly. So far as I have been able to check up his work (which is somewhat outside of my own special line), it is of first rate importance both for the scientist and for the practical breeder, to whose consideration I heartily recommend this little book.

Herbert C. Sanborn,
Dept. of Philosophy and Psychology,
Vanderbilt University,
February 9, 1932.

INTRODUCTION

It is only in poultry that bird infections have ever been studied to any great extent. To adapt these studies to the needs of the canary breeders is the chief object of this book; but since certain diseases are common to both canaries and poultry, it is hoped that those interested in the latter may also be benefited by the results of the experiments here presented.

Some of the chapters are extraneous to what might be expected from the title, but they are included in order to make the book more helpful and complete. Methods of care and feeding of canaries that will keep them in good health might well belong in a book on diseases, since prevention of impaired condition of his birds should be the first aim of every owner. It also seems fitting that the chapters on injuries and insects should be included, as birds afflicted by them need treatment if they are to be useful units in an aviary.

The notes on pathogenic organisms do not contain a description of all the germs attacking birds and there is no reason to think that they are complete even so far as the canary is concerned. They are not given with that intention but in an endeavor to show the breeder that while scientific investigations, carried to the full limit of possibility, may task the knowledge and ingenuity of the most skilled investigators, it is possible often to obtain practical results with the simplest of equipment. I hope this book will stimulate the scientific study of canary diseases which has been so much neglected.

Those who are interested in this subject and wish to follow it farther are referred to the "Diseases of

INTRODUCTION

Domesticated Birds,'' Ward and Gallagher, Macmillan & Co., 1927; ''Principles of Microbiology,'' Moore, Macmillan & Co., 1912, the extensive literature of the Bureau of Animal Industry and the Hygienic Laboratory, as well as of the various state experimental stations that have done extensive work on the diseases of poultry.

The list of drugs by no means contains all those that have been suggested for use on canaries, but I think that it is reasonably complete; and it certainly contains suggestions for the treatment of every disease that I have ever found in a canary. I do not find one-tenth of the drugs listed necessary in treating my own birds, or even the experimental birds I use, but have tried to make the list comprehensive enough to permit the breeder to use it as a reference when the question of the action of any drug is under consideration. In its preparation I have consulted the U. S. Pharmacopœia, 1905; Merck's Index, 1907; and Blumgarten's Materia Medica, 1929; and for more complete information the reader is referred to these works.

CONTENTS

Chapter I
ANATOMY

Sections
- The Skeleton 3
- The Muscles 9
- The Circulatory System 10
- The Lymphatic System 14
- The Nervous System 15
- The Digestive Tract 16
- The Organs of Respiration 21
- The Urinary System 23
- The Reproductive Organs 24
- The Skin 25
- The Feathers 26
- Incidentals 27

Chapter II
FEEDING

Sections
- General Discussion 29
  - Hemp Seed 29
  - Milk 31
  - Green Food 33
- Minerals 35
  - Salt 35
  - Iodides 37
  - Phosphates 38
  - Sulphur 39
  - Silicon 40
  - Iron 41
- Vitamines 42
  - Vitamine A 43
  - Vitamine B 44
  - Vitamine C 45
  - Vitamine D 46
  - Vitaminosis D (Rickets) 47
  - Methods of Supplying Vitamine D to Canaries 48
  - The Reproductive Vitamine 49

Chapter III
MY OWN METHOD OF FEEDING

Sections
- List of Foods 51
  - Rape Seed 51

CONTENTS

List of Foods, Continued
   Canary Seed 52
   Hemp Seed 52
   Tonic Seed 53
   Mineral Food 53
   Bread 53
   Green Food 53
The Singing Male 53
Birds in Flight Cages 54
Breeding Birds 54
Egg Food 55
General Management 55

Chapter IV
SOME FEEDING EXPERIMENTS AND FORMULAE

Sections
   Meat 58
   Formula No. 1 58
   Formula No. 2 58
   Formula No. 3 59
   Cold Boiled Potato 59
   Formula No. 4 60
   Pratt's Buttermilk Baby-Chick Food 60
   Dried Egg Yolk 60
   Mineral Food Formula 63
   Color Food 63
   Tonic Seed and Song Restorers 63

Chapter V
INSECTS AND PARASITES

Sections
   Mosquitoes 66
   Lice and Mites 67
   Mites 68
   Scaly Leg Mite 69
   Feather Mite 70
   Gape 71

Chapter VI
THE MOULT

Sections
   The Physiology of the Moult 74
   Indigestion Due to Improper Feeding During Moult 76
   Baldness 78
      The Moult 79
      Kind of Baldness 81
      Treatment of Baldness 84
      The Moulting of Breeding Stock 86

CONTENTS

Chapter VII
INJURIES AND ACCIDENTS
Sections
- Broken Bones in General 89
- Broken Wings 89
- Broken Legs 92
- Egg Rupture 95
- Prolapse of the Uterus 96

Chapter VIII
SEPTIC FEVER
Sections
- General Discussion 97
- Classification 103
- Etiology 104
- Symptoms and Course of the Disease 105
- Treatment 109
- Psittacosis 111

Chapter IX
APOPLECTIFORM SEPTICEMIA IN CANARIES
Sections
- General Discussion 113
- Symptoms and Lesions of the Gastro-Enteritic Form 115
- Acute Hemorrhagic Form 115
- Immunity 117
- Treatment 117

Chapter X
INFECTIOUS NECROSIS OF CANARIES
Sections
- Etiology 119
- Symptoms 119
- Morbid Anatomy 119
- Treatment 120

Chapter XI
HEMORRHAGIC SEPTICEMIA IN CANARIES
Sections
- General Discussion 122
- Etiology 122
- Fowl Cholera in Canaries 124
- Symptoms 124
- Morbid Anatomy 125
- Immunity 126
- Treatment 126

CONTENTS

Chapter XII
NESTLING DIARRHOEA
Sections
General Discussion 128
Symptoms 129
Causes 130
Treatment 130
Thrush 131
Bacillery White Diarrhoea 131
    Etiology 132
    Symptoms and General Characteristics 132
    Morbid Anatomy 133
    Treatment 134

Chapter XIII
AN UNIDENTIFIED DISEASE OF CANARIES
Sections
Characterization 135
Etiology 135
Symptoms 136
Morbid Anatomy 136
Treatment 137

Chapter XIV
ASPERGILLOSIS IN CANARIES
Sections
General Discussion 139
Morbid Anatomy 141
Symptoms 141
Diagnosis 142
Treatment 142
Some Interesting Cases 143
Infection 145

Chapter XV
MY BIRD IS DEAD
Sections
An Introduction to Diagnosis 146
The Observation of Symptoms 146
Pathology 149

Chapter XVI
BACTERIOLOGY
Sections
Taking Specimens 152
Taking the Cultures 155
Blood Cultures 159

CONTENTS

Chapter XVII
SOME ORGANISMS PATHOGENIC TO BIRDS

Sections
   Bacterium Pasteurella Avium 162
   Streptococcus of Apoplectiform Septicemia 163
   Bacterium Sanguinarium 165
   B Paratyphosus B 166
   Organism of Infectious Necrosis 170
   Organism of Sporadic Pneumonia 173
   Bacillus Coli 176

Chapter XVIII
DRUGS

Sections
   List with Notes on Their Mixtures and Use......................................180
   Rules for Doses 223
Index 230

CHAPTER I

ANATOMY OF CANARIES

THE SKELETON

The skeleton of a bird is a grotesque sight to ordinary eyes, but to those of the engineer it is a thing of great beauty, for nowhere else in nature does one find a better application of engineering principles. Lightness of weight, strength, and flexibility are obtained in a perfect manner. The ilium is very highly developed. Another perfection of construction is the clavical (wish-bone) which forms a natural spring and prevents the powerful impulses of the flight muscles from forcing the wings to strike each other or dislocating the shoulders. It takes up the momentum of the wing perfectly and thus makes flight possible.

The Skull. The skull of a canary has a brain-case almost as thin as paper to which the upper mandible is attached by a cartilaginous (gristle-like) process. The lower mandible is attached to the skull by means of a joint back of each ear, from which a long narrow jaw-bone (submaxillary) extends to the beak proper into which it grows as a continuous process. The occipital bone at the back of the skull ends in a nipple-like process that fits into a deep cavity in the atlas bone (the first cervical vertebra). In the fore part of the skull, between the eyes and the beak, are the nasal sinuses. The opening of these cavities runs upward into the nasal cavity. For this reason there is no natural drainage of the sinuses into the throat as is the case in mammals. When these processes become infected during disease, an artificial opening between the eyes often results.

The Vertebral Column. The number of cervical vertebrae varies in different species of birds, and different investigators often ascribe different numbers to the same species. This is due to differences of opinion as to where the cervical vertebrae end and the thoracic vertebrae begin. I consider that the division should be made where the neck ends between the shoulders, the place where it breaks off even with the body when in a cured specimen it is bent back until it parts from the body. This allows a canary eight cervical vertebrae.

The anterior extremity of each cervical vertebrae has the articular surface concave from side to side and convex from front to back. This with the peculiar attachment of the skull mentioned above assures great flexibility and accounts for the bird's unusual power of moving the head.

The thoracic vertebrae (the ones to which the ribs are attached) are eight in number in the canary. The first is articulate (has the power to move), and there is a joint between the sixth and seventh thoracic vertebrae. The last two are fused solidly to the lumbar vertebrae to form the anterior portion of the ilium. The second, third, fourth, and fifth thoracic vertebrae are ankylosed. There is a certain limited articulation between the fifth thoracic vertebrae and the sixth. The principal movement of the back occurs between the sixth and seventh vertebrae.

The lumbar and the sacral vertebrae, together with the last two thoracic vertebrae, are fused into a single bony mass which is called the ilium.

ANATOMY

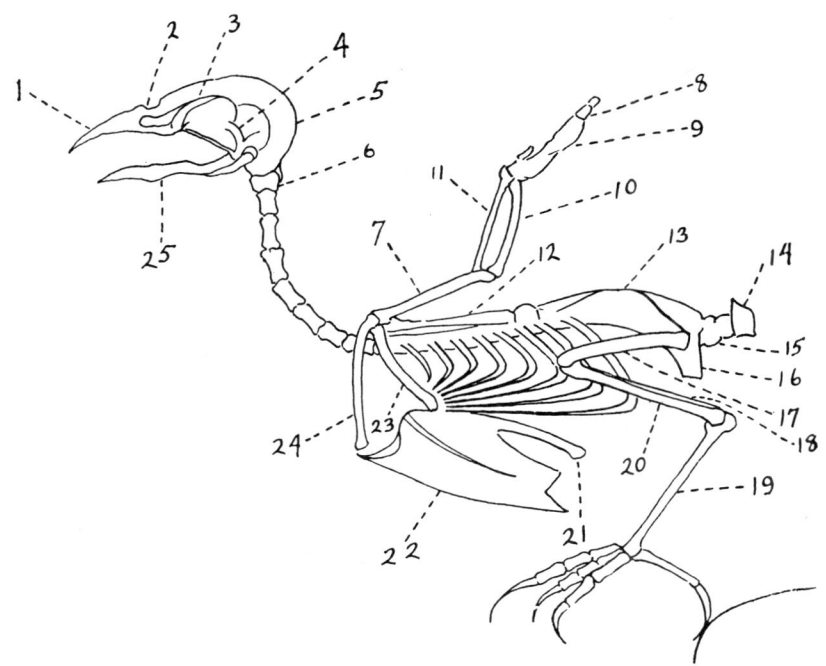

SKELETON OF CANARY

1. Incisive
2. Nasal
3. Lachrymal
4. Quadrate
5. Occipital
6. Atlas
7. Humerus
8. Phalanges
9. Metacarpus
10. Ulna
11. Radius
12. Scapula
13. Ilium
14. Pygostyle
15. Ischium
16. Pubis
17. Femur
18. Fibula
19. Metatarsus
20. Tibia
21. Patella
22. Sternum
23. Coracoid
24. Clavicle
25. Mandible

There are four coccygeal vertebrae, the first three of which are much shorter than the other vertebrae. The last one turns upward and is much larger than the others. It has a broad thin spin or plate rising dorsally (toward the back of the body) on the median line. This plate forms a septum dividing the oil gland and the mass of tissue that carries the tail feathers. This process is called the pygostyle.

The Ribs. A canary has eight ribs on each side of the body, which articulate with the thoracic vertebrae and with the sternum. The first rib does not reach the sternum.[1]

The ribs in a canary do not sweep around the thoracic cavity as they do in mammals. They radiate from the spine in graceful arcs slanting toward the posterior. The superior ribs end on a line slightly anterior to the lungs and even with the anterior extremity of the pubis. They are there joined with the inferior ribs which radiate fan-like from the sternum, each one forming a more or less acute angle with its superior rib. There is no joint between the two parts of the rib, but they are so thin that this angular structure permits considerable motion.

The Sternum. This bone is highly developed in birds, for it has to provide surface for the attachment of the powerful flying muscles as well as support for the thoracic and a portion of the abdominal cavity. It is concave on its inner surface and convex on its

---

[1] I have examined the body of one roller in which the last two ribs were heavier than the others and extended back along the sides of the abdomen under the thighs. In this body only five ribs were connected to the sternum. In the body of a Yorkshire canary before me at this moment seven ribs are connected to the sternum. I have not been observant enough to say whether this difference is a matter of breeding (which is not probable) or whether the roller studied was a freak in this matter.

ANATOMY

outer surface. Besides the median line on the external surface is a deep ridge called the keel on account of its resemblance to the keel of a boat. On each side of the sternum is a long bony process that runs parallel with the lower portion of the ribs and ends in a wide flat expansion. In some birds there are two of these processes on each side, but in the canary there is only one. From the forward border of the sternum extends a small spine to which the furculum (wishbone) is connected by a ligament. This bone is said to contain air sacs, but I could not find any such cavities in the sternum of the canaries I examined. It may be that the openings were too small to be noticed by the naked eye.

The Wing Bones. The shoulder contains three bones; the scapula, a saber-shaped bone extending back over the ribs; the clavicle (the arm of the wish bone) connecting with the sternum through the furculum; and the coracoid, a heavier bone, connecting directly with the sternum at a point between the wish bone and the ribs.

The first bone of the true wing is the humerus. This bone, which is the heaviest bone in the wing, articulates in a cavity formed by the terminations of the coracoid and the scapula.

The next section of the wing, corresponding to the forearm in a human being, is composed of two bones. The heavier is called the ulna and the lighter, the radius. The ulna is slightly curved, while the radius is almost straight. They are united at their ends by bands of ligaments.

The last division of the wing is the metacarpus. This is formed by a fusion of the bones which in a later stage of evolution become the hand of man. It is to this bone that the primary flight feathers are attached. Just below the connection with the radius on the outer surface is attached a small bone (phalange) that corresponds to the human thumb, while at the end are three small bones which are the rudiments of two fingers.

The coracoid, humerus, and ulna contain air cavities.

The Pelvis. The pelvis in birds is composed of three bones as is the case with mammals, but with the difference that the pubis which completes the pelvic arch in mammals is incomplete in birds and does not unite in front. The largest bone of the pelvis is the ilium. This bone is fused with the last two thoracic vertebrae and with all of the lumbar and sacral vertebrae. The ilium is highly developed, and on its inner surface contains large ridged cavities into which the kidneys fit snugly. This gives these organs a complete covering of bone on the dorsal surface which is in some places thicker than the skull. The ridges on the inner surface of the pelvis give the bone at once great strength and little weight. The ischium, which is solidly attached to the ilium, forms part of the sides of the pelvis. The pubis attached to this extends downward; but, as already mentioned, does not unite as it does in mammals.

These three bones meet at the hip joint to form the cavity in which the femur articulates.

The Leg. The largest bone of the leg is the femur. This articulates in a ball and socket joint at the hip and in a hinge joint at the knee, where it is connected with the tibia and the fibula. The former is the large bone that carries the weight; the latter corresponds to the radius in the arm but is rudimentary and incomplete, tapering off to a fine point at its lower extremity. At the ankle the tibia is connected with the metatarsus which is the first bone of the foot, often called the scaly, or lower, leg. It is a long round bone ending in a thumb and three fingers. The thumb in a canary has one bone and a claw. The inside finger has two bones and a claw, while the other two fingers have three bones and a claw.

THE MUSCLES

The muscular system of birds in general corresponds regularly to that in mammals; and as the muscular system in a canary is of little importance in the treatment of diseases, there is nothing to be gained from a detailed discussion here.

There are two flight muscles on each side of the breast. These are called the greater pectoral and the lesser pectoral muscles. The former is the largest muscle in the bird's body. Its attachments extend from the clavicles down over the sternum, where it is attached to borders of that bone and to the lateral processes, as far down as the lower ribs. This is the muscle that depresses the wing in flight. It is connected by a tendon to the head of the humerus.

The lesser pectoral muscle which elevates the wing lies beneath the greater and originates on the outer surface of the sternum, in the trough between the keel and the sternum proper. It is also attached to the clavicles and to the membrane between the clavicles and the sternum. Its tendon passes through the process called the foramen triosseum (shoulder joint) that is formed by the union of the scapula, coracoid, and furculum, which acts as a pully, and is then attached to the humerus opposite the attachment of the great pectoral tendon.

The diaphragm in a canary is only slightly developed, and it does not form a complete partition between the thoracic cavity and the abdominal cavity as is the case in mammals.

Some birds, especially those which in a wild state make little use of the wings, have white breast muscles, but this is not the case with the canary. All the muscles of this bird, when it is in a healthy condition have the deep red color of normal muscular tissue.

THE CIRCULATORY SYSTEM

The Heart. The heart, which is the central organ of the circulation, is a powerful muscular pump whose function it is to force the blood through the arteries. The heart of a canary is situated well forward in the thoracic cavity, is conical in form and reddish brown in color. It contains four cavities. The two upper cavities have very thin walls and are called auricles; the two deeper cavities have thick, heavy walls formed of a multitude of bands and layers of muscles interwoven in such manner as to give great strength. These so-called "smooth muscles," found also in other internal organs, differ from the striated muscles that supply the power of locomotion in that they are not enclosed in sheaths of serous membrane. These two deep, thickly walled chambers are called the ventricles.

Blood flows into the right auricle from three veins that collect it from the various parts of the body, and into the left auricle from two veins, one coming from each lung. When the auricles are full, the valves between the auricles and ventricles open and the blood

ANATOMY

flows into the ventricles. The auricles are contracted and the ventricles are expanded. At this time the heart is said to be in disystole. When the ventricles are full of blood, the valves between them and the auricles close while those between the auricles and the veins entering them open. The auricles relax while the ventricles contract with a powerful impulse. The used blood in the right ventricle is forced out into the pulmonary artery where it is carried to the lungs for aeration. The blood in the left ventricle is forced out into the aorta where it is carried to all parts of the body. This contraction of the ventricles and expansion of the auricles is called systole. One disystolic movement and one systolic movement constitute one complete heart beat.

The right auriclo-ventricular valve in birds differs from that in mammals. In the latter this valve is formed by three triangular pieces of heavy, tough tissue that close upon each other in a sort of pyramid. In a bird this opening is closed by a fold of muscle which fits closely over the opening and prevents the blood from being forced back into the auricle. In other respects the heart of a canary does not differ from that of a human being. The muscular portion of the heart is enclosed in a thin serous sac called the pericardium.

Bacteria may sometimes lodge and grow on the inner surface of the heart valves, thus producing inflammation which results in a deformation of the valve such that it cannot close tightly; and when the heart goes into systole, some of the blood is forced back into the auricles. This condition is called endocarditis.

During acute diseases blood, serum, cells, or a jelly-like exudate may collect in the heart sac, greatly distending it and interfering with the beating of the heart. This condition is called pericarditis and is a common condition in septic fever, cholera, and pneumonic diseases in canaries. Besides the two conditions just mentioned the muscles of the heart itself may suffer necrotic changes.

The Arteries. On leaving the heart, the aorta gives off a large branch that passes up the neck. This can be plainly seen where it runs over the crop. The aorta itself makes a U-shaped turn and extends down the body close to the back bone as far as the coccygeal, giving off numerous branches throughout its course.

The Veins. The blood is returned from the body to the heart by means of a single large vein, while that from the head and neck is returned by means of two veins that are connected with each other at the base of the skull.

The Blood. The blood of a bird like that of a mammal is composed of a straw-colored fluid, or plasma, in which the cells float. There are several kinds of cells found in the blood. The red cells are by far the most numerous in normal blood, but they are accompanied by white cells, or leucocytes, in the ratio of about 125 red cells to each white one.

Red corpuscles in birds differ from those in most mammals in that they have a nucleus. They are thin oval discs about twelve microns long and seven wide. When stained with Giemsa, the neuclei take a deep blue stain and the discs a light pink. The function of the red cell is to carry oxygen to the muscles and carbon-dioxide from the muscles to the lungs.

There are five kinds of leucocytes or white blood cells found in birds, two of which are shown in the cuts.

ANATOMY

The function of these cells is that of scavengers, that is, they devour and digest any bits of protein matter as well as invading bacteria found in the blood. These cells seem to live a relatively independent life. They may float with the blood stream but have also the power to move against the current or to quit the blood channels at will and to move out into the tissue. Their bodies are so flexible that they can migrate, so to speak, through the pores in the walls of the blood vessels. They wander out through the tissue, invading nerve sheath, organs, muscles, etc., no doors being closed to them. When they find bacteria, they devour and digest them with great vigor. Sometimes these cells will devour so many bacteria that they actually burst.

As mentioned above there is normally only one white cell to each 125 red ones, but in disease these white cells multiply with great rapidity. In some instances the ratio of white to red cells has been found to be as high as one to seven. This is the case in such diseases as typhoid and infectious leukemia. In recent years the enumeration of the white cells has been widely used in diagnosing deep-seated infections in human beings, a small amount of blood being drawn from the ball of a finger, and the relation of white to red cells determined by examination under the microscope. Any departure from normal relationship is an indication that infection exists, and the comparison of one day's white count with the next will tell definitely whether the disease is progressing or being overcome by the resistance of the body.

THE LYMPHATIC SYSTEM

The lymphatics in birds differ from those in mammals in that the bird has no superficial lymphatics. The skin of a bird plays no part in the regulation of the heat of the body. There is no extensive vasimoter system as there is in human things; so that a superficial lymphatic is not required. A bird maintains the heat of its body at a constant temperature by the position in which it holds its feathers. When the feathers are held loosely so that they inclose considerable air, they become highly insulating and prevent the loss of bodily heat. This with shivering and exercise gives the bird ample protection against cold. The only protection that it has against heat is by holding the feathers close to the body and panting. The wings are held out from the body when the bird is warm and drooped when it is cold. The loss of water from the extensive respiratory system and the lessened insulating power of the feathers when held close are ample protection against heat when the bird is in the wild state; since, due to the high temperature of the bird's blood, he meets few natural temperatures when in the wild state that will distress him; and when he does meet them he uses his wings to move to a more agreeable climate.

The lymphatics in birds are deep-seated and contain few glands. The most important ones are situated in the neck, one on each side, at the point where it passes between the clavicles. They are somewhat smaller than a maw seed when they are healthy, but I have found them as large as number 12 shot, or larger, and containing a gritty deposit in cases of tuberculosis.

ANATOMY

THE NERVOUS SYSTEM

The Brain. The brain is the central organ of the nervous system. The brains of birds are very highly developed, but they differ from those of mammals in that the cortex or outer surface of the cerebrum is smooth instead of corrugated and convoluted as is the case in the cerebrum of mammals. The brain of a bird is creamy white in color during health. The relative size of a bird's brain to its body varies greatly in different species. It is greatest in such birds as owls and the small flying birds. One-fourteenth of the weight of a canary's body is brain matter. The best human ratio is about one to forty-five.

The cerebellum is located at the base and to the rear of the skull. The lateral lobes of the cerebellum in birds are very small; while the optical lobes, which are placed at the sides, are correspondingly large. The optic nerve is as large as the spinal cord indicating the great importance of sight in the life of a bird. This is to be expected, for a bird in the air that cannot see and recognize safe perching places is really badly off. On the other hand the olfactory lobes are smaller than in mammals, so that it is even a matter of great doubt whether birds actually have the sense of smell. (Cf. experiments of Darwin, Audubon, Rouse, Strong, etc.)

The Spinal Cord of a canary extends straight down the vertebral column from the skull to the coccygeal. It contains two expansions: one is located in the last cervical and first two thoracic vertebrae, controlling the movements of the wings; the other is in the sacrum, controlling the actions of the legs. Those given off on the anterior side of the spine (the visceral or front side—really the bottom side of a bird's spine) are motor in function, that is, they are the nerves that carry the movement commands to the muscles. Those nerves that enter dorsally, that is, toward the surface of the back, are sensory in function.

THE DIGESTIVE TRACT

The alimentary system in birds differs greatly from that of mammals. There is no provision for mastication of food in the mouth, as birds have no teeth. Many birds swallow all of their food whole; but this is not the case with certain of the small seed eaters, which do chew their food to some extent, inasmuch as they remove the husks of many seeds. The lack of teeth is made up for by a gizzard which functions as a very powerful food grinder.

The Mouth. A canary's mouth is triangular. The lower mandible fits into the upper, and the edges of the last third of the lower mandible turn inward, forming a chewing surface that the bird uses in shelling its seed and in masticating food for its young. The edges of the upper mandible are sharp throughout. The roof of the mouth is formed by a hard palate that does not meet on the median line, that is, there is no soft palate as in mammals. The tongue is long, narrow, ending in a sharp point. At the base of the tongue is a slit with which the trachea is connected and through which the bird breathes. A short distance in front of this slit there is a slight offset in the tongue mounted by two small projecting processes which the bird uses in forcing food back into the opening of the esophagus (gullet or food tube) through which it is carried to the crop. The esophagus passes down the right side of the neck.

ANATOMY

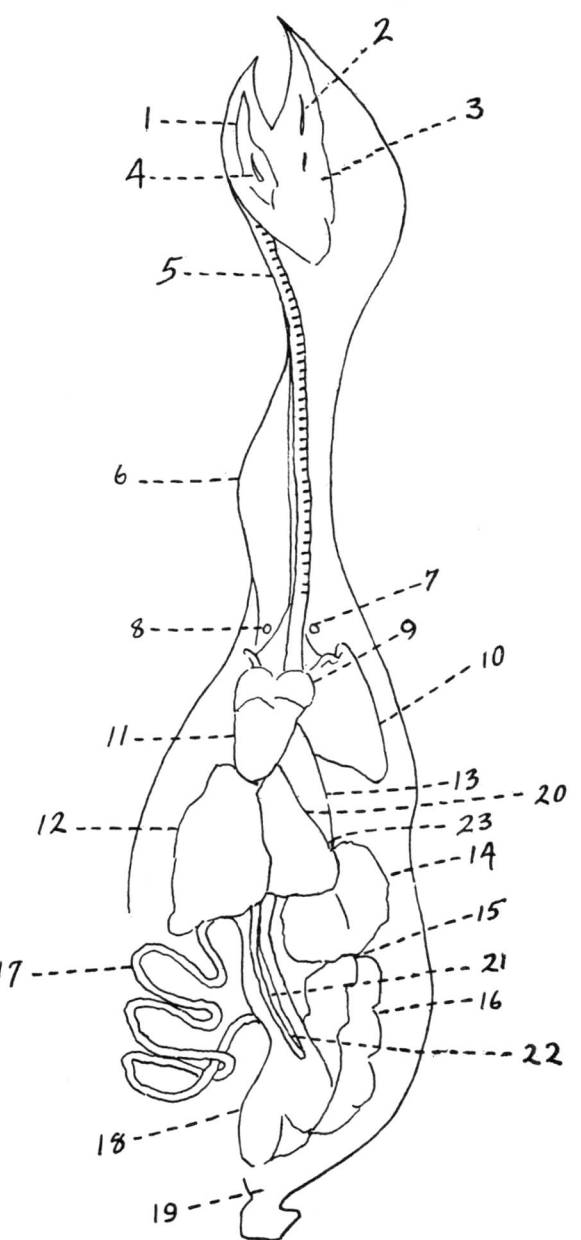

VISCERA

1. Tongue
2. Cleft
3. Common orific of Eustachian tubes
4. Upper larynx
5. Trachea
6. Esophagus and crop
7. Lymphatic glands
8. Bronchial tubes
9. & 11. Heart
9. Auricles
10. Lungs
11. Ventricals
12. Liver
13. Proventriculus
14. Gizzard
15. Oviduct
16. Kidney
17. Small intestines
18. Cloaca
19. Vent
20. Spleen—under liver, not shown
21. Duodenum
22. Pancreas
23. Gall bladder

The Crop. The crop in a bird is an expansion of the esophagus. In a canary it is situated on the right side of the neck about half way between the mouth and the point where the esophagus enters the thorax. The function of this organ seems to be that of soaking the food in digestive juices and softening it as well as acting as a place for storage. It is well supplied with blood from the carotid artery. During the breeding season the surfaces of the crop secrete a thick creamy substance which is mixed with the food that the old birds give to the young. The crop and the esophagus are formed by four layers of tissue: an outer serous membrane, a layer of longitudinal muscles, a layer of circular muscles, and an inner mucous layer. Food in the crop is mixed and passed on to the stomach by means of a circular movement performed by a wide circular muscle. Secretion into the crop is from the alveolar glands of the esophagus and from the mucous glands. This organ has no special glands for the secretion of gastric juices.

The Proventriculus (or Glandular Stomach). At the lower end of the esophagus there is a pronounced bulge. The wall becomes thickened and contains a large number of glands that pour out gastric juice which is mixed with the food as it passes through this organ. There is only a slight expansion in the inner diameter of the food tube at this point and no space for the storing of food during digestion as there is in the animal stomach. The food is fed down slowly from the crop, and the only function of the proventriculus seems to be that of supplying gastric juice. Between the proventriculus and the gizzard there is a valve which regulates the passage of food into the gizzard. When the food contains irritating matter that causes acute in-

ANATOMY

digestion, this valve closes and prevents the passage of the food into the gizzard.

The Gizzard (ventriculus bulbosus). The gizzard or stomach in a canary is a large, thick-walled, muscular organ lying on the left side of the upper portion of the abdominal cavity. The muscles of this organ are very dark in color, but they are bound into position by heavy bands of silver-gray connecting tissue that pass over their surface; and these are often overlaid with bunches of yellow fat, so that the organ appears light-colored.

The muscles of the gizzard are not only the darkest in the bird's body, but they are by far the most powerful, exceeding in the power of their contractions even those of the heart; but like the heart muscles, they are not provided with sheaths of connecting tissue. These muscles are attached to a strong membrane, and to this in turn is attached the inner lining of the organ.

Inside the gizzard is found a cavity of considerable capacity which regularly contains numerous bits of gravel and other hard substances in addition to food. The inner lining of the gizzard is a thick, tough, corrugated membrane, some portions of which are almost as hard as horn. The organ is so shaped that the two surfaces of this lining on opposite sides of the cavity may be pressed together and moved with a circular, grinding motion, one against the other. It is this motion of these horny surfaces against each other, aided by the sand, that enables the bird to reduce the hardest seed to an almost fluid state, and to extract from it the last particle of nutriment.

The Intestines. The first portion of the intestines into which the food passes is the duodenum. This is the longest loop of the intestine and also has the largest diameter. It extends toward the lower portion of the abdomen for some distance and then returns on itself close to the starting point. Between these two parallel sections is situated the pancreas, that pours a secretion into the duodenum, called pancreatic juice, which has the power to digest starch. The gastric juices provided by the proventriculus digest only protein foods.

After leaving the duodenum the diameter of the intestine becomes gradually smaller, the tube undergoing a number of convolutions before the rectum and the cloaca are reached. In some birds there are two blind guts (ceca), or appendices, leading off from the point where the intestines join the rectum. A canary does not have these; neither do sparrows or other small seed-eating birds.

Just inside the vent there is a large bulge in the tube. This is about the same size and shape as the glandular stomach and is called the cloaca. It serves as a common receptacle for the discharge from the bowels, the ureters, and the oviduct in the female and the *vasa deferentiae* in the male. It is divided into three portions: the rectum enters the upper or first portion; the ureters and the genital ducts open on the sides of the second portion (one oviduct of the female enters from the left side). The material from the intestines and the ureters is collected in this sack to form the dropping, which is voided through the vent.

The Liver. The liver in a canary is, when in a state of health, dark brown in color. It is attached to the spine and receives a large blood supply from a short artery connected with the descending aorta. It lies on the right side of the abdomen and has two lobes. The right lobe is considerably larger than the left with a gall bladder attached to the lower portion of the inner surface. The left lobe has a bile duct that connects directly with the duodenum. The bile secreted by the liver digests fat.

The Spleen. This organ is not, properly speaking, a part of the digestive system. It is a reddish-brown organ situated under the upper edge of the left lobe of the liver. In a canary it is about one-fourth of an inch long and one-sixteenth of an inch in diameter when the bird is in health. The normal color is slightly lighter and more reddish in cast than that of the liver. The exact functions of the spleen are not understood; but its location and normal appearance should be well understood, for changes in the spleen are very common in disease and in some cases they are very important for diagnosis.

THE ORGANS OF RESPIRATION

There is considerable difference between the respiratory system of birds and that of mammals, for in addition to lungs birds are provided with a number of air-sacs, tubes, and air cavities widely scattered throughout the body.

The Nostrils and Upper Air Passages. A canary's nostrils consist of two small round holes situated on the line where the horn of the upper mandible joins the skin of the head. The openings are usually protected by a fringe of short feathers that cover them. The two nasal chambers are separated by a wall (septum) which is in part of bone with the remainder of cartilage. The cavities open into the mouth through a common orifice, a cleft in the hard palate. The air enters the trachea through what is called the upper larynx. This is a small slit-like opening in the back part of the tongue, provided with two lips that close the openings during the passage of food through the pharynx. This upper larynx has no vocal chords and has no function in the origin of the voice sounds. It is often said that it does not function in the song of the bird, but I am inclined to doubt that statement. I believe that this flexible opening through which the sound must pass has a most important influence upon the tone quality of the song, since it is probably involved in the production of certain overtones.[2]

The trachea is a long tube extending from the larynx in the back of the mouth to the syrinx situated in the upper part of the thoracic cavity. It is formed by a large number of cartilaginous rings that are held together by a membrane of connective tissue. These rings serve to prevent the tube from collapsing.

The syrinx, or true voice box, is a rather complicated organ in singing birds. A number of the trachea rings are enlarged and consolidated to form a relatively large cavity, which is provided with membranes that vibrate when the air is passed over them and which are provided with muscles that regulate their tension and thus control the voice. The syrinx in the best roller canaries is much more highly developed than that found in birds singing only the common canary song.

The bronchial tubes divide just below the lower opening of the syrinx; one tube runs to each lung and enters its anterior extremity (most forward part). The bronchi are provided with rings between the point where they separate and the points where they enter the lungs. These rings are not complete, however. About one-third of the surface of the circumference

---

[2] Just as is the case with the pharynx in human beings and other animals. (Editor's Note.)

ANATOMY

of the tube is composed of a membrane which forms its dorsal wall.

The Lungs. The lungs in birds are much smaller than in mammals. They are triangular in shape, of a spongy texture, and are bright pink in color when in health. It is the pale pink lung that is healthy; the dark lung is always diseased. The lungs fit closely to the dorsal surface of the thoracic cavity and fill completely the spaces between the ribs. This gives the back of the organ a grooved surface.

The Air Sacs. In addition to the lungs a bird is supplied with air sacs. These are composed of a thin, transparent membrane of two layers, an outer serous surface and an inner mucous surface. They are supplied with air by means of tubes running from the lungs and the bronchi; and they, in turn, supply tubes that carry the air to the cavities in the various bones. There are nine of these air sacs in the abdominal and thoracic cavities. It sometimes happens that a bird either through illness or injury ruptures one of the air tubes. The disorder may arise from malnutrition or degeneration of the tubes through infection. When that occurs, the skin fills up with air and the bird becomes helpless. This air may be drawn out by puncturing the skin with a needle but it soon gathers again. I have not seen enough of such injuries to know whether healing is possible or not.

THE URINARY SYSTEM

A canary has two kidneys, each supplied with a ureter lying along the ventral surface and draining into the cloaca. Each kidney has three lobes and fits snugly into the cavities in the pelvis, one kidney lying on each side of the spine. These organs are reddish brown but the color is duller than that of the liver and much duller than that of the spleen. They are not, however, divided into tufts as are the kidneys of animals. The ureters and uriniferous tubes can be easily distinguished by the white urates that they contain. The kidneys are very soft and it is difficult to remove them without rupture.

THE REPRODUCTIVE ORGANS

The Male. The male canary has two testicles situated in the abdominal cavity near the anterior edge of the kidneys. They are round or oval in shape, of a light cream color, and vary in size from that of a small rape seed to that of a hemp seed. The average size when in breeding condition is about that of a No. 6 shot. Old males will sometimes have one testicle as large as a BB shot and the other very small. Each testicle is provided with a *vas deferens* (excretion duct) which leads to the uro-genital portion of the cloaca. These ducts make a number of convolutions along their course instead of running straight as do the ureters which they follow closely in direction. Each duct opens on a small raised papilla on the side of the cloaca. Each papilla has a plexus of blood vessels and is erectile during coition.

The Female. The female canary has a single ovary and oviduct situated on the left side of the abdominal cavity. As a rule, the right ovary and oviduct do not develop, but there are cases in which they are present in a rudimentary form. The ovary is attached to the spine in the left sub-lumbar region adjacent to the anterior extremity of the left kidney. The ovary itself is pearly-white in color and is firmly attached to the side of the spinal column. On the ventral surface are a

ANATOMY

large number of rods on the ends of which are ova in various stages of development. The active ovary of the hen has an appearance suggestive of a bunch of grapes, excepting that the grapes are usually of one size while the ova are graduated in size.

The oviduct is a large, convoluted, membranous tube in which the egg is developed. It is blue-gray on the outside and has five divisions: first the infundibulum, which is funnel shaped and receives the ovum; second a section devoted to the secretion of albumen; third a section devoted to the secretion of shell material; fourth the uterus, where the formation of the shell is completed; and fifth the vagina, which opens into the cloaca through an orifice provided with a sphincter muscle.

This sphincter prevents the contents of the cloaca from gaining entrance to the oviduct. Sometimes this muscle becomes torn by the passage of a large egg, and there is danger of waste matter entering the oviduct and causing peritonitis. The bird in such cases becomes very weak and will be found at the bottom of the cage unable to stand and breathing very rapidly. If left without treatment she will die in a very short time. About ten drops of a solution of Stroud's Antiseptic, two grains to the ounce of water, fed into the beak with a medicine dropper will overcome this infection and allow the bird to be back on her nest in twelve hours or less. There is no other known treatment for this condition, so far as I am aware.

THE SKIN

A canary's skin is devoid of the sweat and oil glands found in many animals. Instead of these, it has one large oil gland located on the upper side of the coccyx. This gland is spherical in shape, divided on the median line by a septum and imbedded in a mass of fatty tissue. The opening of the oil duct is raised above the surface and is shaped like a nipple. The bird draws oil from this gland and uses it for water-proofing and dressing the feather. Should the **gland be destroyed, the bird is very apt to die before or during the next moult.**

THE FEATHERS

The feathers of a bird are a complicated modification of the skin cells. In the initial stages of the growth of a feather, a small portion of the skin is first drawn inward to form a small pit (feather follicle), and it is from the bottom or side of this pit that the feather itself forms; first as a minute projection that rapidly turns into a quill which projects above the surface and is filled with blood. It is from the outer end of this quill that the feather grows. The feather itself consists of a central shaft which has a hard glazed surface on the outside and a white pulpy mass inside. On each side of the shaft is a fan, or web, composed of fibers, which, when in good condition and healthy are rendered adhesive by the action of the oil so that an air-tight fan is formed. While this is generally true of almost all feathers, it is especially true of the flight feathers. The outer ends of the body feathers follow this same construction, but the lower part of the web of the body feathers is likely to have the fibers of the web less well developed than those on the outer part of the feather, each one curling and twisting in a different manner and thus forming a fluff or down that has great heat insulating properties. Canaries have less of

---

[3]By oiling and massaging I have effected cures. (Editor's Note.)

ANATOMY

this down than most other birds. The body feathers on a canary are not uniformly distributed. There is one row of feathers that extends from the back of the head to the tail. Another row starts under the beak and extends about two-thirds of the way down the neck where it divides. Each division turns sharply toward the wing for a short distance, then makes a slight turn in toward the median line, which it does not reach, and then turns outward and backward along the abdomen, ending under the thigh. There are body feathers on the head, wings, legs, and around the vent and tail; but the abdomen, back, and sides of the body are naked with the exception of the three rows of feathers mentioned, although there may be a few scattered, downy pin-feathers in these naked areas. This arrangement of the feathers is the same as that of the plates on the reptile from which the bird evolved, and in the bird has been perfected so as to offer a minimum of air resistance during flight. The feet of a canary have no feathers, but here the original scales have been retained.

INCIDENTALS

The incubation period of a canary is about twelve and a half days. It may vary from eleven and a half to fourteen according to temperature and the care that the hen gives the eggs. I have had eggs hatch and the birds live after sixteen days of incubation, but they had been hindered in their development by chilling.

The normal temperature of a canary in health may vary from 104 to 108 degrees F. The usual temperature of a canary in breeding condition is 107½ degrees F.

The pulse, counted by watching the movement of the carotid artery, (this is easily done when the crop is full by bending the feathers back away from the crop so that the artery is plainly visible where it passes over the crop) is about 150 per minute but in certain conditions may reach a rate as high as 300 per minute.

Respiration varies considerably. The average rate for a healthy bird while at rest or during sleep is from 80 to 100 per minute. The sitting hen breathes a little slower except when frightened. A frightened bird will breath over 200 times per minute. A bird suffering with the pneumonic form of septic fever (called "contagious bronchitis" in poultry) will often breathe 280 times in a minute and the average rate for a bird with the fever is between 150 while at rest and 200 while moving around. A hen with peritonitis will breathe over 300 times per minute and the pulse will be nothing but a feeble flutter, too rapid to count.

CHAPTER II

FEEDING

Some Researches Into the Influence of Different Food On Health, Growth, and Reproduction

General Discussion

Every beginner with canaries is puzzled by the wide range of feeding methods advocated by different breeders and different writers on the subject. One breeder swears by hemp seed; the next one swears at its mention and tells of the harmful effects that are sure to follow its use. Another tells what good results come from the use of bread and milk, but states also that he has always been bothered by having soft moult in his flock, and that his hens go out of breeding condition very easily. There are furthermore, those that ridicule the use of green food, crediting it with being the cause of all the ills to which the canary is heir. With the idea of settling in my own mind just what the effects of these different foods are and of learning the grounds for these many differences of opinion, I have been experimenting and keeping records on this subject for some years. What follows is an account of some of my experiments and the conclusions that I have drawn from them.

Hemp Seed

Experiment. Six hens were fed hemp seed while making eggs. They were given the seed crushed in the egg food. This egg food was made of one hard boiled egg, enough dry ground bread to make it crumbly yet moist (about twice as much bread as egg by bulk). A mixed tonic seed, containing about 20 kinds with lettuce seed, niger seed (commonly sold as thistle seed), maw seed and flax seed as a base, was added in amount equal to the bread used, and to this was added 10 drops of pure cod liver oil. For hens fed on hemp the crushed seed was mixed into this food in the ratio of one part hemp seed to two parts egg food. Six other hens were mated at the same time and these were given the same food before the hemp was added to it. None of the birds in this test had ever had any direct sunlight. Green food, principally dandelion and grass, was given to all alike.

Results. In the first round the most noticeable difference was that the eggs from the birds fed on hemp seed had better shells. The mottling on the eggs was more red than that on the eggs from the hens having no hemp in the diet. In the second round the eggs from hens receiving hemp seed were much more hatchable than those from the hens not having hemp. In the third round several of the hens that had had no hemp laid soft shelled eggs.

The chicks raised from the hens fed on hemp seed were larger and grew better than the others, but there was a high death rate from the sixth to the tenth day, which made the production record of the two groups nearly equal. The hens that had been fed hemp did not go into moult easily.

This experiment was repeated in three separate years. Different grades of hemp were used. Some birds were given direct sunlight, others were given hemp with the cod liver oil, still others were given hemp seed, but neither cod liver oil nor direct sunlight. Hemp was fed to the hens anywhere from the tenth day to the day that they hatched. The results of all of these tests would be dry reading, but they led to several conclusions that are hardly in accord with generally accepted opinions on this subject.

Conclusions. The conclusions from all of these feeding tests are that stale hemp is poisonous to nestlings even when it is not stale enough to be harmful to the old birds; that fresh hemp is not harmful to birds of any age and may be fed in large quantities from the day that the chicks hatch without endangering the lives of the young or the health of the old birds; that this seed is rich in the reproductive vitamin E and in the sunshine vitamin D, but that it does not contain enough of the latter to support growth and prevent rickets throughout the breeding season; that it is lack of these two vitamins that causes exhaustion of the old birds from breeding. The most unlooked for result was that old birds, given an unlimited supply of hemp while the hens were making eggs, and while the young were being fed, did not get over-fat. Young birds in flight would get as fat as butter on this diet and it would soon kill caged singers. It was found that caged singers would not get over-fat on one-fourth teaspoonful of this egg food daily, however, but would come into loud ringing song. The evil narcotic properties often ascribed to hemp seed were not found in any of the tests that I have made. I am forced to conclude that they are largely imaginary.

Milk

"Everybody knows that milk is good for canaries." Well, I had not known it, although I had been breeding canaries for three years at the time an old breeder told me this. The next season I fed bread and milk to all of my hens feeding babies, and to all of the young. Things went splendidly for a while; the hens fed well, the babies grew very fast. The young were all big, strong looking birds with plenty of feathers. For some unknown reason mortality was high, and the old birds seemed to have no resistance to disease. The hens went into moult easily and a number died in the moult. Next year, still feeding bread and milk twice each day, I had 85 in soft moult at one time. This called for some more experimenting. I made tests with the bread and milk just like those with the hemp seed. The tests did not take so long as those on the seed, for every bird given milk as a regular part of its diet sooner or later went into soft moult. Eight more birds were set aside for tests. They were caged separately. The diet was of rape and canary in equal parts, plenty of green food, two days each week a little egg food, and on the other days a little tonic seed. Four were given a small piece of bread and milk every day, the other four were not given milk in any form. All eight were given direct sunlight every day that the weather would permit. This was continued from September until March. Of the four birds given no milk every one lived through the winter and made a good breeder the next season. Of the four that were given the milk every one was out of song before January. One died; the other three developed swollen feet and soft moult. By discontinuing the milk and putting these three birds on the same diet as the others, two of them were brought into song and were later sold as singers when they were two years old; but not one of the four started with produced fertile eggs the first season following the test, and one was kept until it was three years old and could never be brought into perfect health. It would sing a little, but not enough to permit me to sell it, and it was sick every time the weather changed. This bird was at last killed and dissected. Calcifications were found in the lymph glands of the neck and several calcified nodules were found in the intestines and liver. These were large, almost as big as a rape seed. There were no small nodules. It was concluded that this bird was recovering from tuberculosis at the time it was killed, though the nodules were not tested for tubercle bacilli.

A comparison of my breeding records for the three years when milk was used and for those when it was not used gave me all the information that was needed, in connection with the experiment given above, to convince me that milk is an item that should be omitted from the birds' diet. I have found that the birds grow as well on dry bread moistened with water, and a plentiful supply of fresh green food.

Green Food

Grass is the real staff of life of all terrestrial creatures. Even the animals that live on the flesh of other animals are indirectly dependent upon the supply of grass for the supply of the animals they eat. The green of the grass and the red of the blood are closely related iron compounds, and without this organic iron no warm blooded creature can live. The reason is simple: this compound is the one that carries the oxygen that keeps up bodily heat. Grass, and other green foods, also contain large quantities of vitamin A. This vitamin is necessary to life, and a diet not containing it will in every case be followed by a diseased condition, which in birds is called nutritional roup; for it begins with symptoms closely resembling that disease.

These observations apply to all warm blooded creatures, but it should not be necessary for any intelligent person to consider such things in attempting to determine the needs of the canary. In the wild state the seeds of grasses are the canary's natural food; their tender leaves spice his diet; and he builds his home of their fibers. Milk may give the vitamin A if the cows were fed on green grass; meat will give him the iron that he needs; a nest may be made from strings or hair; but these are likely to yield anything but a healthy, happy canary.

The dangers from green food are caused by depriving a bird of it and then giving him some cultivated plant that is far from fresh (often the stale leaves of lettuce or spinach), when he is so starved for it that he will over-eat on food he would not touch if he were given his choice. Furthermore, *bleached* lettuce, cabbage, etc., have few or none of the vitamines possessed by the natural green leaves. I have never found any harmful effects to follow the constant use of wild green food.

One other problem connected with green food is that of determining the kind that is best for the birds. Every breeder has his own answer to that question, and barring poisonous weeds and hot-house greens, it really makes little difference with the birds so long as they get plenty of it fresh. Dandelion is a very good plant to use, but I have found that no one plant really fills the bill. Lawn grass, with all the weeds that grow with it, including dandelion, dock, pepper grass, and a host of other plants that thrive in a neglected lawn, is about the best thing that I have found in the way of bird greens. The next time you cut your lawn try some; or better, spade out a piece of fresh sod for your birds and see what they do to it. It you have any eggs hatching and will watch the hen closely, you will see her dig into the sod and get the black loam from around the roots and feed it to her young. If you will look a little later, you will see the black showing through the skin of their crops. Chicks that start life on this black loam dirt do not die easily from indigestion. Fully one-third of the ailments I am called upon to treat would be unknown if plenty of good grass, roots, dirt and all, had been included in the bird's diet.

MINERALS

It is generally recognized that all birds need more lime than is contained in the ordinary diet, and it is for this reason that almost all breeders in this country keep cuttle-bone, egg shell, or both, constantly before their birds; but these articles, valuable as they are, do not always contain everything that the birds need in this respect. They do very well in some localities. The caged singer may live on them for years as his only source of minerals outside of those he gets in his food and water, but there are other rarer minerals for which there is a great need only during the breeding and moulting seasons. It is the lack of these minerals that is responsible for the exhaustion from which our birds often suffer during the breeding season and the moult that follows.

Salt (Sodium Chloride) is a necessity in the blood of all warm blooded creatures. Its functions are to maintain the physical properties of the blood at the point where it is possible for the red cells to function in the carrying of oxygen, and to permit the double decompositions by which the body breaks up the potassium salts (which are the principal minerals found in vegetable matter) into their elements, so that they may be used by the animal body. When you sweat and drink ice water on a hot day, the exhaustion that follows is due to the lack of salt in your blood.

When either man or animal lives exclusively on vegetable food for any length of time an irresistable craving for salt is developed. Cattle will travel hundreds of miles in search of this necessary substance. The Eskimos also travel long distances to the sea in order to get it.

Poisonous Effects. When salt is taken in too small amounts to keep up the proportion necessary in the blood, water is permitted to accumulate in the tissue and the red cells of the blood expand until they are ruptured and destroyed. When too great an amount of salt is present in the blood, water is withdrawn from the cells and absorbed by the salt so that they shrivel up and are no longer able to function. This last is not a serious matter in the case of animals, for the excess of salt creates a craving for water and the salt is promptly carried off through the skin and kidneys. Birds are not so fortunate. They have no pores in their skin and their kidneys are designed to handle urates in a thick pasty state, and not to care for an excess of water. The result is that letting a bird that has been starved for salt overeat it is apt to cause death. Chickens are sometimes killed accidentally by eating rock salt which they seem to take for gravel.

I have found that birds that have always had plenty of salt will not overeat of it, or of the food containing it. I have given experimental birds salted peanuts as a part of their regular diet without any ill

FEEDING

effects, but it was necessary to give this food only in small quantities until the craving was satisfied. The two best ways to give salt are either by putting a small pinch in the egg food every day or by using it in the mineral food mixture.

Iodides. (Potassium or Sodium Iodides.) When the Great Lakes basin was first opened up for white settlement, it was discovered that, notwithstanding an abundant food supply and good climate, sheep could not be raised in the district. Old sheep brought in did fairly well, but the young were always born dead or died shortly after birth. This state of affairs went on until a farmer drilling a well for water struck by accident a vein of salt water with a very bitter taste. This water, being of no value, was permitted to run out on the ground. And right here animal craving showed its superiority to human intellect. Sheep and cattle broke down the fencing around the well and drank of the bitter water; and the sheep for the first time produced normal young. Analysis of the water showed that it was rich in the salts of iodine. The first step had been made in the discovery of the cause of goiter in human beings. It had long been known that people who lived on the sea coasts, and lived largely on sea food, did not have goiter, but no one had ever found the reason for it. All sea water and sea food is rich in the iodine salts, and such people had been getting as much of it as they needed.

In my early breeding experiences I in one year had ninety per cent or more of the young for three rounds dead in the shell or dying shortly after hatching. After frantic efforts to stop the loss, and tests designed to find out the cause, I at last thought of iodide deficiency as a possible cause. I added four drops of potassium iodide to each quart of drinking water and raised two full rounds from the same hen that had given me only dead chicks up until that time. Since then I have always made potassium iodide a part of my bird's mineral diet. This is an element that is necessary only in very small quantities. For cattle and sheep only one ounce to the 100 pounds of mineral food is necessary, and for birds only three ounces to 100 ounces of mineral food. People living on or near the sea coast will not be troubled by this lack of iodides in their birds' diet, or in their own, and there are now many inland cities that put into their drinking water the correct amount of iodides for human needs; but in other inland localities both human beings and birds suffer for lack of this element. Wherever there is an undue proportion of birds found dead in the shell, iodide deficiency should be considered as one of the possible causes.

Phosphates. (Potassium, Sodium and Calcium Phosphate.) Phosphates are necessary for the life and growth processes in both animals and plants. In the mammal and the bird the bone structure is composed of calcium phosphate. Seeds and all plant matter are rich in potassium phosphate. A large number of physiological processes require the presence of sodium phosphate. Now the normal animal or bird with a normal supply of salt has no trouble in getting from the food supply all and even more phosphates than are needed, by changing the potassium phosphate in the food into the sodium and calcium phosphate required. There are, however, conditions under the strain of breeding where the body loses this capacity. In such cases phosphates added to the mineral food are of great value. Thirty per cent phosphate in the form of steamed bone meal

FEEDING

added to the mineral food along with 2 per cent of neutral sodium phosphate will be found to give good results. In old persons and old birds the power to metabolize the phosphates is sometimes lost, and such cases are treated with a tonic preparation known as Syrup of Hypophosphites. This is a very good tonic for a bird that is badly run down from disease, over breeding, or other mistreatment; but with good care it is not apt to be needed. Syrup of Hypophosphites is usually given along with cod liver oil, as the vitamine D contained in the oil helps in the metabolism of phosphates.

Sulphur. Sulphur is used in large quantities during growth and reproduction, as it is a constituent of albumen of which the softer tissues of the body are largely composed. The white of egg contains a large amount of sulphur, so that birds in the breeding season, fed on egg food, never suffer from lack of sulphur. The feathers also contain a great deal of sulphur and the indigestion that is so common in pet birds following the moult, is mostly due to the fact that they have not been fed enough egg food during the moult to supply the sulphur needed for feather production. Many breeders have the idea that raw sulphur in the form of flowers of sulphur is of value in the bird's diet. A small amount of such sulphur can be utilized by the body, and in some cases of sickness it may be of some value. I do not think, however, that there is any good reason for its continued use.

The judicious use of fresh egg food, or other meat foods (animal proteins) will supply the bird with all the sulphur needed. Most breeders understand this need, but many of the complaints that they receive, from those who buy pets from them, are due to the fact that they fail to impress this need of the moulting bird upon their customers.

Silicon. Another need of the moulting bird is the element silicon. Silicon is one of the most abundant of all the chemical elements. Its compounds make up 87 per cent of the earth's crust. The ones with which most persons are most familiar are quartz, white sand, and agate. These are nearly pure forms of silicon oxide. This element enters into plant and animal life in very small quantities, and the inorganic minerals are so insoluble that they are unavailable for plant and animal use. It is only in the outer coating of straw and of some grains and seeds that silicon is found in any great quantities in the vegetable world; in the animal world its use is confined almost exclusively to the construction of hair and feathers. For these it is an absolute necessity in the diet. And of all the seeds that we feed to our birds the only one that contains usable silicon in sufficient quantities is canary seed. Type bird breeders who care nothing about song and use the very best grade of mammoth canary to make up from four-fifths to nine-tenths of their birds' seed diet, have little trouble from lack of silicon. This is not the case with the roller breeder. He is set on song. He knows that canary seed will make the birds sing loudly, and hence reduces the amount of canary seed and increases the amount of rape seed in the diet. And almost every year he wonders why it is that some of his birds do not feather well, and that others develop indigestion toward the end of the moult. I have found that while the singing roller can be reduced to a seed diet almost exclusively of rape seed, the breeding bird must have at least 50 per cent canary seed and the moulting bird about 75 per cent canary seed if the best results are to be expected.

Iron. I pointed out in a previous discussion of this subject that the organic iron compound which is responsible for the green color in vegetable matter and the one that is responsible for the red color of the blood are very closely related. There is no danger that the well-treated bird, that has plenty of green food every day of his life, and egg food as it is needed, will ever suffer from the want of iron. But where a bird is not well treated it is just as apt to become anemic as a human being is. I am sure that many cases of "going-light" are due to the fact that the birds are fed too much head lettuce and apple instead of good grass and weeds. The bird that does not get enough iron loses weight and becomes very weak, just as the anemic human being does. I have found that in such cases two drops of I. Q. S. tonic given to each ounce of drinking water along with the necessary foods will do wonders for the bird. This should not be given for more than one week at a time. If given much longer the symptoms of strychnine poisoning will develop.

This list does not include all the mineral elements that enter into the bird's physical economy, but it does include those for which there is apt to be a lack in the diet. I have tried to show in each case the necessity for the element treated and the best way in which it can be supplied. Unfortunately, the living body's power to metabolize minerals is very largely dependent upon certain obscure food elements known as vitamines, the sources and functions of which must now receive some consideration.

VITAMINES

Vitamines are rare chemicals present in living matter which exert a vital influence upon certain of the life processes. They are formed by nature under circumstances that are not well understood in most cases; and their chemical nature, physical properties and mode of action are likewise very obscure. We do not know what they are; we do not know all that they do, or why they do it; we do not know, with one exception how to make them; but we do know that they are each necessary to the development of certain special life processes, and that when they are not present in sufficient amounts illness, deformation, and death follow. We know that each vitamine is responsible for certain definite functions since these functions fail when they are not present. We know that they are to be found in certain foods since these foods cure the pathological conditions which are the result of their absence or deficiency.

Vitamines have been designated by letters in place of names because we do not know enough about the substances of which they are composed to justify naming them. Some of the disease conditions due to vitamine deficiency were known generations before the existence of these substances was suspected and have special names, but they are now spoken of in general as *vitaminosis*. The letter by which the vitamine that prevents the condition is known is added to designate which vitamine is lacking. There are only four of the vitamines that are at all well understood and they are designated A, B, C and D. That there are several others is known, but with the exception of the one that influences reproduction, not enough is known about them to justify a discussion.

Vitamine A

Wherever plants are growing in sufficient sunlight to produce a green color vitamine A is being manufactured. It is not manufactured under any other circumstances as far as is now known. When the plant is dried the vitamine is stored in the part that retains a green or yellow color. These colors are due to iron salts which may or may not have a part in the manufacture of the vitamine, but are certainly distinct from it. This is known from the fact that it is possible to destroy the vitamine without destroying the coloring matter.

Vitamine A is found in all green leaves. The outer leaves of head lettuce are rich in it but not the inner white leaves. The skin of an apple is rich in vitamine A but the pulp contains very little. Oranges are very rich in vitamine A, as are also yellow carrots, yellow corn, and, I believe, sweet potatoes and fresh rape seed. It is not found in white corn or white potatoes. It is found in eggs and milk only when the cows and hens producing them are fed on foods containing it. Vitamine A is also found in liver tissue, in cod liver oil, and possibly in some other oils. It is not destroyed by drying, but it deteriorates as the dried foods become aged.

Vitaminosis A is the disease which always develops when this food element is not present in the diet in sufficient quantities. The symptoms of the early stages of the disease are exactly the same as those of the beginning of a cold or of roup. There will be a discharge from the eyes and nostrils, and in the ordinary course of events bacteria will invade these lesions and from there gain admittance into the blood. The kidneys lose the power of eliminating uric acid from the blood and that may lead to swelling of the feet. If the birds do not die of other secondary causes, at the time of death, the inside of the esophagus will be found covered with pimple-like nodules, which are due to enlarged glands. Uric acid may be present in the blood up to 40 or 50 times the normal amount, and there may be deposits of white uric acid crystals within the body, often upon the surface of organs. Birds suffering with this ailment have little resistance to other diseases and are very apt to fall victim to the first infection that comes along. They have a strong predisposition toward pneumonia. Old birds will withstand a diet deficient in vitamine A for a longer time than young birds. The latter may die in from 4 to 8 weeks, while old birds may live as many months, but in all cases death is the result if the diet is not corrected.

Vitamine B

Vitamine B is found in the outer coverings of all grains and seeds. It is not found in grain or seed products where the outer covering has been removed, as in the case of polished rice and white flour. It is never lacking from the diet of old birds living on a seed diet. This vitamine seems to act upon the nerves.

Vitaminosis B is the disease that is due to a deficiency of vitamine B in the diet. Beri-beri, a disease that is more or less common in rice eating countries, is due to a lack of the vitamine B in the diet of polished rice. Birds fed upon polished rice or white bread will develop the same disease. The symptoms are the same in both human beings and birds. They are: digestive disorder, loss of weight, nervous twitchings and spasms, and the loss of control of the limbs. In the bird, a drawing back of the head and continual nervous spasms usually precede death. As has been said, the bird on a seed diet will never suffer for lack of vitamine B, but the body is able to store this vitamine in much smaller quantities than is the case with vitamine A. The disease develops very quickly, sometimes within four or five days, when the vitamine is removed from the diet. The only cases of this disease that I have seen in canaries have been due to the feeding of too much bread, or bread and milk, and not enough seed, or to the use of prepared foods deficient in vitamine B. It is hand-fed canary chicks that suffer mostly from *vitaminosis B*. They are usually fed upon bread, egg yolk, and green food, and even where whole wheat bread is used, there is some danger of this condition developing along about weaning time. The bird draws the head back, falls on the side, and goes into one nervous spasm after another. The only treatment needed is to supply the needed vitamine B. This is best done by crushing some rape seed and removing the hulls by blowing and sifting. A single feeding of this ground rape will relieve the more serious symptoms. If all breeders hand-feeding chicks will use some of this fresh ground rape daily, if only for a single feeding, they will not be troubled with this disease.

Vitamine C

Vitamine C is present in all fresh green food. Its function is to keep away the condition known as scurvy in human beings. Birds seem to have the power to manufacture this vitamine. Poultry experiments have shown that birds supplied with a reliable amount of vitamine A can get along without fresh green food. There are so many other good reasons for feeding green food to the canary, however, that no breeder should be misled into thinking that because poultry have been shown to be able to get along without this one element present in green food that that is sufficient reason for omitting green food from his canary's diet. It is very likely that the canary can get along without having this vitamine in his food, for a time at least. Vitamine C is the only one of the vitamines that does not resist drying. For that reason alone one must assume that any creature that can live on dried seeds throughout the winter months either has the power of supplying this vitamine for itself or storing it in the body in quantities sufficient to last throughout the winter. Man himself does the latter, where the winters are not abnormally long.

Vitamine D

Vitamine D, the sunshine vitamine, is produced by the action of ultra-violet light upon certain chemical compounds that are widely distributed in the tissues of both animals and plants.

Ultra-violet light is light having a wave length so short that it cannot be seen by the human eye. It is very active upon a great many chemical compounds. This activity is made use of in photography. It is the action of the ultra-violet light that causes tanning and sunburn when the skin is exposed to the summer sun. This component of the sun's rays cannot pass through ordinary window glass to any great extent.

It has long been known that children living in the slums where they did not receive enough direct sunlight and poultry grown under glass were alike subject to a disease of the bones known as *rickets*. The bones lack the lime and phosphates necessary for perfect development. This was first thought to be due to a lack of lime and phosphates in the diet, and it has been proven that the condition can be brought about by withholding these important elements. It was soon shown, however, that in many cases of rickets no shortage of lime or phosphates existed in the diet. This fact led to the discovery of the part played by direct sunlight in the metabolism of calcium (lime) and phosphates. It was also discovered that cod liver oil was capable of supplying this much needed vitamine in the absence of direct sunlight. Recent discoveries have shown that it is possible to treat many food stuffs with ultraviolet light and increase the vitamine D content far above that normally present in cod liver oil. Experiments on baby chicks have shown that from 10 minutes to one hour in the sunshine every day, the time depending on the strength of the sun, is enough to permit normal growth. There are now on the market certain electric lights that are thought to supply this much needed ultraviolet light. They have been largely used upon poultry, but I have not heard of anyone's testing them out on canaries.

Vitamine D is primarily a growth vitamine. Adults, either human or avian, can live for a considerable length of time on a very limited supply of Vitamine D without any serious injury to the health, unless it be a slight lowering of the resistance to infection. This is not, however, the case during moult and the period of reproduction. Growth, whether it is the growing of feathers, the production of eggs and young, or the growth of bones and body tissue in the young chick, seems to make demands upon the body's supply of this vitamine.

Vitaminosis D (Rickets)

The first manifestation of deficiency in vitamine D in canaries is the falling off in production. The hen produces soft, thin-shelled eggs, light in color. Many of the eggs are clear; in others the chick develops but fails to hatch and is found dead in the shell. Of those chicks that hatch most will die in the first few days and of those that live until they start to feather many will develop true rickets. The body loses its soft pink color and becomes darker. The skin is dry and the body seems withered. The legs seem far too long for the body and the bones, instead of being the soft spongy pink of healthy bones, become brown, dry and hornlike. The head seems to grow smaller and the beak takes on an eagle-like hook. The bird dies as a rule between the eighth and fourteenth day. This condition can develop where the hen is a good feeder and herself has had plenty of direct sunlight if the food is totally lacking in this vitamine. It seems that the young bird, if normal, comes into life with enough vitamine D to last about eight or ten days.

Methods of Supplying Vitamine D to Canaries

The simplest way of supplying birds with this important element is to keep them in an aviary, one portion of which consists of an outdoor flight. The indoor flight is almost as good if the windows are fitted with cello-glass instead of the ordinary kind of window glass. The birds may be carried into the open air for a sun bath every day, some form of sun lamp may be used, or they may be fed on foods that give them this necessary element. The choice of method to be used will depend a great deal upon the convenience of the breeder. It is not the method but the result that counts. And an examination of most breeding plants will show that the birds get this element from several distinct sources, any one of which might be sufficient in itself, but which together furnish an adequate supply.

Fresh hemp seed, though not in itself containing enough vitamine D to keep breeding birds in condition, often contains enough to prevent rickets and to maintain growth in the chicks from the time that they start to feather until they leave the nest. Egg yolk, if the hens laying the eggs have had sufficient direct sunlight, will be found rich in vitamine D. Cod liver oil has long been used to supply this element. It is a reliable source of supply, but has the drawback of making the birds over fat. Then many birds do not like the taste of it and will not eat food containing it. Recently the makers of Bond Bread have adopted a newly discovered process which incorporates this element in their bread. As this bread has been upon the market for only a short while I do not think that it has as yet been used in making egg food for canaries. It is possible that it would be to the breeder's advantage to give it a thorough trial. For if this vitamine can be given in the egg food in a form lacking the objections of cod liver oil, it will greatly simplify the breeder's problem and assure a larger proportion of strong healthy chicks from a given number of eggs.

The Reproductive Vitamine

I am not familiar with the experimental results of other investigators concerning a reproductive vitamine, but in my own breeding experiments the existence of such vitamine is clearly indicated. I mentioned some of my experiments with hemp seed in the August, 1930, issue of the *Roller Canary Journal and Bird World*. I found that even though all the vitamines listed above and all the food elements mentioned in my other articles on feeding were provided, nevertheless, birds that were fed on hemp seed or sunflower seed while making eggs produced better colored eggs with stronger shells and maintained a much higher rate of production than was the case with birds deprived of these seeds.⁴ The logical conclusion from these experiments is that there is in these two seeds, and perhaps in many other substances, a vitamine that has a marked influence on reproduction in canaries. My experience indicated that milk in the diet destroyed this influence, and that old seeds or cooked seeds were lacking in the influence of fresh seeds to a considerable extent, although seeds that were rancid enough to cause the death of four day old nestlings still possessed enough of the vitamine to permit the hens fed on it to produce hatchable eggs, while the controlled hens could not produce hatchable eggs.

So far in this discussion of feeding, I have given the principles underlying correct diet, and some few suggestions on the application of those principles, but I am afraid that the average breeder may find this treatment of the subject rather vague. In my next chapter I shall attempt to combine all of these principles into a practical system of feeding which will insure that the birds get the things they need with the least possible effort on the part of the breeder. I will not attempt to maintain that this system is the best ever invented or that it is "fool-proof," but only that it is the one that has given me good results.

---

⁴For ten years I fed dogs on a diet of beef, oatmeal and rice, cooked together, and from as many as eight to ten bitches raised no puppies at all. Then upon the advice of Dr. C. C. Little, I changed to nothing but raw meat and the bitches became pregnant and had puppies. (Editor's Note.)

CHAPTER III

MY OWN METHOD OF FEEDING

Before going into the details of my feeding system I will give a brief list of the foods used and a few remarks concerning each.

Rape Seed. This seed comes in many grades. Those listed on the market are: Holland rape, small summer black rape, small red German rape, large sweet rape, dwarf Essex rape, and still other names that are applied to mixtures that are part rape or not rape at all, but are sold as such. Many of the mixtures contain wild mustard seed, turnip seed, cabbage seed, and a host of others. I have planted some samples that contained at least twenty different kinds of seeds, all sold as rape.

The best grade of rape, if you can get it, is Rubson. This is a dark reddish-brown seed, with a slightly purple cast. The seed is about the size of a No. 12 bird shot. When taken into the mouth and chewed, it has a taste slightly like nut. It is not hot or bitter, and if stale is almost tasteless.

Good Rubson is very hard to get, and the next best seed is the small red German summer rape. This is about twice the size of a maw seed, about the size of a No. 16 shot. It has a sweet nutty taste and should be composed of seeds of nearly all one color and one size. There should be in the sample no hot seeds that bite the tongue when they are chewed. It should be clean and free from dust; and when crushed with a rolling pin on a piece of clean paper, each seed should leave a distinct oily spot on the paper and should roll out into a thin leaf instead of crushing into a powder. If it powders it is old seed that has lost its oil.

All other grades of rape outside of these two mentioned are, in my opinion, unfit for bird seed. Because a seed is called "Large Sweet," it may insure that it is large but does not insure that it is sweet. Your own tongue will tell you that. Any time you are in doubt, plant the seed and see what grows.

Canary Seed. This seed, too, comes in a number of different grades. For type birds the grade needed is the Mammoth Spanish Canary. For rollers I think that good Morocco canary is the best; but regardless of which size seed is used, canary seed must have the following qualities. The shell must be a bright straw color; shiny, not dull. It must not have a greenish or a brownish cast. When you put your hand into the sack, it must sink into the seed with ease and come up free from dust. The seed must grow when planted. When a Mason jar is filled half full, sealed up over night, and put in a warm place, the seed must not have a musty smell when opened in the morning.

Hemp Seed. This seed comes in a large number of varieties also. It should be olive colored and about the size of a BB shot. When crushed it should be very oily; and the crushed seed, put in a closed jar over night, should smell and taste very much like English walnuts in the morning. The smell should not remind one of stale butter. There is only one sure test for hemp. Give a hen that is known to be a good feeder and that has chicks under five days old all the hemp that she wants. If the hemp is not good the chicks will all die; if good they will live and thrive. This may seem a hard test to some, but it is the only test that will tell one definitely whether the seed is whole-

MY OWN METHOD OF FEEDING

some. This seed gets rancid easily, and a supply that was good one month may not be good the next. I consider the feeding test well worth the price it costs, because stale hemp will destroy a great many more than one nest of birds if given to a whole flock in the midst of the breeding season.

Tonic Seed. There are many tonic seed mixtures on the market. Most of those put out by breeders are good, whereas most of those put on the market in cans are not likely to be so good, not because they were not good when mixed, but because they are liable to be stale. In another place I shall give formulae for mixing tonic seeds.

Mineral Food. This may be cuttlebone, hen's eggshells that have been boiled to kill the germs of poultry diseases, ground oyster shell, or mixed minerals. The choice will depend a great deal upon the locality in which the breeder lives.

Bread. Bread is used in two ways, and either white or whole-wheat will serve. Some fanciers use crackers or ground cookies and crackers. If breeders live near a cracker factory and can buy the breakage at a low price, this is suitable. The bread, of whatever kind, must be dry enough to grind into a powder. Of course it must not be sour, spoiled or musty.

Green Food. Dandelions, green cabbage, apple, and wild greens of all kinds. Lawn grass is one of my favorite greens for canaries. Green rape plant and canary seed grass raised in boxes are also good.

The Singing Male

The male canary in the singing cage does not need an over rich diet; still, he must have a well balanced ration if he is to stay in health and song. In his regular seed cup he should have nothing but the best grade of small red German summer rape. On the floor of his cage he should have clean sand. In an egg-drawer he should have mineral food. In an extra dish he should get daily one-half egg-drawer of canary seed and one-half egg-drawer of egg food three days each week; of tonic seed, three days each week; of crushed hemp seed, one day each week. In addition he should get some kind of green food every morning. In the winter it is likely to be apple or cabbage, but in the summer it may be grass or dandelion; and he should get all that he can eat.

Birds in Flight Cages

Whether males or females, the birds in flight, except when they are moulting, should get canary and rape mixed in equal parts in the seed dishes. They should have the sand and mineral food and green food daily. I never omit giving any bird green food for a single day. For extras these birds get just the same rations as the singing males, but the extra is given in round canary egg cups that hold one ounce. I allow one cup for each six or eight birds in the flight. This diet is nearly the same throughout the year except that the babies and moulting birds get a little more of the extras and have the egg food every day.

Breeding Birds

For several weeks before they are mated the breeding birds get the egg food daily in small quantities, and as soon as they are mated they get it in unlimited quantities. In their seed cups they have the rape and canary in equal amounts. They get fresh green food twice each day. This continues until the hen sits. From that time until the day before the young are hatched no egg food is given, but they have their green food daily. The day before the young hatch the birds

MY OWN METHOD OF FEEDING 55

are given a small quantity of egg food. The day that the young hatch they have in addition to the egg food, their other regular diet, a piece of dry bread that has been dipped in water. The only changes in this diet are made in the mixing of the egg food.

Egg Food

For making egg food only the best grade of strictly fresh, that is, newly laid, eggs should be used. Cold-storage eggs should be avoided. The egg is boiled from twenty minutes to half an hour and then cooled in cold water. The shell is removed and the egg pressed through a piece of screen wire cloth and mixed with enough bread to absorb most of the moisture. Then it is mixed with half as much tonic seed as there was bread used. (One egg-drawer of mineral food for each egg.) This is the standard mixture. It is the mixture to be made up every morning of the year. For breeding birds when the hen is making eggs, fresh crushed hemp is added equal to the amount of tonic seed used. If I am absolutely sure of my grade of hemp seed, the babies get the hemp in their egg food too; but if I am not sure of hemp seed, none is put in the babies' food until they are ten or twelve days old; and then it is added with caution in order to be sure that it does not cause indigestion. If the birds have had no direct sunlight, five drops of codliver oil are added to the egg food for each egg used.

General Management

Much of the effectiveness of this diet is due to the system of management that goes with it. The diet as outlined for the males would make them fat and lazy if they were permitted to eat and sing all day long. They are opened up and given the light at 8 A. M. They are carried into the air at 11:30 A. M., and permitted to bathe in the sunshine. They are then kept in subdued light from 1 P. M. until 5 P. M., when they are put to bed. The same is true of the males in flight. The females during the early part of the moult are put to bed at 1 or 2 in the afternoon, and during the winter at 3 P. M. Every bird is inspected at least once in two weeks, and the length of the eating day is adjusted to fit the condition of the bird, while the diet remains substantially the same.

The breeding birds are permitted to eat from 5 A. M. until 8 P. M. I do not remove the cock when the hen is sitting unless he causes trouble, and I always let him help feed the young. But during the period of incubation of the eggs, I catch the cock every day at 11:30 and take him out for the sunshine with the other birds that are being taken out. When they come in at 1 P. M., he is put back with the hen. After the young hatch the cock is no longer taken out; but when the hen starts to build her new nest, she is taken out every day until the eggs are laid. By that time the young have left the nest and the hen is taken out entirely and put in flight for two weeks. The eggs are given to some other hen and the cock is permitted to feed the young. At the end of the two weeks the hen is rested and the cock is rather exhausted; the young are weaned. Then the pair is remated and the relative condition of the two birds is such that they are sure to throw an extra large proportion of males. This rest gives the hen a chance to store up the necessary vitamine D and other elements that she needs to avoid exhaustion, and at the same time it permits me to take five or six clutches of eggs from her while she is raising three nests. It puts a lot of work on the male but no more than is good for him when he is only mated

MY OWN METHOD OF FEEDING 57

to one hen; and I have found that it is inadvisable to use more than one hen to the male in cage breeding. In flight breeding three or even five hens can be mated to each male. I know many breeders will disagree with me on this and argue that a hen should be made to raise her brood alone. Maybe she should, but it is those who expect her to and to raise five nests at that, who write to me to find out why it is that their hens do not moult and are no good the second year. My hens are at their best in about their fourth year.

In the application of this system the breeder should always put the eggs of a spotted pair with those of a yellow pair when he fills up the nests; otherwise he will not be able to tell which pair the chicks belong to. I have certain pairs that always throw chicks having distinguishable feather characteristics, and I always keep these in mind when doubling up the eggs.

CHAPTER IV

SOME FEEDING EXPERIMENTS AND FORMULAE

Meat. Early in my breeding experiments I gave considerable thought to the use of substitutes for fresh eggs in raising canaries, for the simple reason that I was not in a situation where I could easily secure fresh eggs. I could not obtain fresh meat either, but I could get the dried and ground meat and bone scraps that are put out by packing houses for poultry feeding. This product is very rich in the minerals and proteins that go to make up the body. It has a feeding power over ten times greater than fresh meat, pound for pound, and so could not be fed in the pure state. I have raised birds on each of the following formulae when flight breeding. I did not have success with them in cage breeding, but they were not thoroughly tested in this respect because after I began cage breeding I was able to get fresh eggs and discontinued the use of dried foods.

Formula No. 1. Finely ground bread one part, sifted meat and bone scraps ½ part, yellow corn meal ½ part, finely sifted oat meal ½ part, ground rape seed 1 part, olive oil 3 per cent, or one-half ounce to each pound of the mixture. Some hens would not eat this mixture. Those that did raised fine, healthy birds so long as it was made up fresh every week. After this period the rape seed would get rancid; and either the hens would refuse it or it would kill the chicks.

Formula No. 2. Same as No. 1 but with the rape seed left out and 30 percent of crushed hemp added fresh every day. It was also tried with about 20 per-

FEEDING EXPERIMENTS

cent of tonic seed mixed into it and about 20 percent of hemp added fresh each morning. On this mixture I raised some of the finest birds I ever saw and they gave me some wonderful production records. The young were big boned and healthy but the food injured the old birds. It was far too stimulating, but at the time I tested it I did not know enough about birds to realize that I was making the food too rich for them and over breeding them.

These foods had enough oil in them to keep them from being dusty and were fed dry.

Formula No. 3. Meat and bone scraps 1 part, whole wheat flour sifted to remove the coarse bran 1 part, yellow corn meal 1 part, dry ground bread 3 parts, one-half teaspoonful of baking powder to each quart of the mixture. Water is added and the mixture is worked up into a thick dough and baked in a slow oven till thoroughly cooked. After the food is cooked and cooled it is cut into thin slices and dried and then ground up to about the size of rape seeds. It is best fed moist, and many birds like it and will raise wonderful chicks on it. At the time this food was used I had some losses from fits. At that time, not being familiar with the cause of fits, I considered the food responsible for them and discontinued the experiments with it.

Cold Boiled Potato. This is a food that all hens are very fond of and will always feed to their young in large quantities. I have had many hens raise their nests of birds on boiled potato and seed, and raise every bird, too. This food has grave dangers in warm weather, for it will become mouldy and sour in a very few hours. Almost all chicks fed on boiled potato suffer from diarrhoea after leaving the nest. They do not die of it, however.

Formula No. 4. Dry ground sponge cake 2 parts, fresh grated carrots 1 part, tonic seed mixture 1 part, crushed hemp ½ part. This was fed to young over five days old. The old birds had in addition dried egg yolk before them. Some hens raised fine birds on this mixture, but at this time some of my hens had young afflicted with rickets and hatched very few of their eggs. Fleischman's yeast, one-half cake for each ten hens, and two drops of cod liver oil for each hen were added to this mixture, and for the rest of the season the birds did well. There was, however, a high death-rate among the old birds during moult. This is not to be wondered at since they were mated in December and bred constantly until July, some of the hens laying as many as 40 eggs. The fact that some of them raised full nests in July after such a strain speaks well for the food mixture, after the vitamine deficiency was corrected.

Pratt's Buttermilk Baby-Chick Food. A number of hens were fed on this food and raised good chicks on it as one of the sources of protein (it was not the only source, for these birds had bread and milk daily and some of the meat food). The food was sometimes fed moist and sometimes dry. All hens that ate much of this food developed swollen feet and enlarged livers. They were worthless for breeding thereafter.

Dried Egg Yolk. Dried egg comes in three forms. One form contains both the yolk and the white. It has a putrid odor and the birds will not eat it. One form is composed of pure yolk, sun-dried. This is very oily and if kept closely packed it will get rancid quickly. If mixed with enough dry ground bread to absorb the oil it will keep fairly well. It is best fed dry and with the oily bread sifted out and thrown away and

FEEDING EXPERIMENTS

an equal amount of fresh ground bread added just before feeding. This is a very rich food. Birds feeding it should have potato or moist bread to use as bulk food. This diet is deficient in vitamines, and if they are not added from some other source the birds will not do well. For birds getting plenty of direct sunlight, fresh green food, and enjoying plenty of exercise, that is, birds in free flight, no better food can be found. There is the danger, however, that the sun-drying process will not always kill the germs of poultry diseases. I have never had disease in my own flock from this source but have had several cases reported to me.

The dried yolk of hard boiled eggs is one of the best foods that I know of for raising strong, healthy chicks if it is carefully prepared and made fresh once each week. If it is permitted to become stale or if it is permitted to pack down when it is drying so that the center does not get enough air to dry thoroughly and rapidly, its use is sure to lead to apoplectiform septicemia. It seems that the streptococcus that causes this disease is well distributed in nature and has a preference for egg food as a substance to grow in. This food just mentioned, when well prepared and mixed fresh each week, is much safer than the ordinary egg food in hot weather, however. Like the sun-dried yolk (I did not have a single case of fits in my young birds while using the sun-dried yolk) this food is so rich that the birds must have plenty of moist bread to feed along with it. It is not advisable to mix the yolk with the bread or to feed it moist.

Grape nuts, cream of wheat, corn flakes and most other breakfast foods can be fed to canaries as soft foods if the birds are given the necessary vitamines from other sources.

There are some canaries that will eat insects if given the chance to try them, but most of them will not try the insects until they see another bird eating them. If the breeder will take the trouble to teach his canaries to eat insects and will then give them a plentiful supply of this food when they are breeding, he will find that his baby birds grow as never before. You have all seen the little brown moth that so often makes your seed wormy. Once in my early breeding I had been feeding a nestling food that I had bought. The birds did not like it at all and would only pick out some of the seeds in it and throw the rest out of the saucer. The saucer was filled up again and the refuse left where it fell. Sometimes when I could get the eggs, egg food was fed in the same saucer and the pile of refuse had gotten 3 inches deep and 18 inches in diameter. Then came a nest and I had no nesting food and no eggs, nothing but seeds and potato, and not always the potato. I expected the birds to die. They did not. The hen would spend most of her time working this pile of refuse over. I thought she was finding something in it she could eat and so did not bother it. The chicks were the fattest and grew faster than any I had ever seen. The hen weaned them and built another nest. Then one day when visitors were expected, I cleaned up my house and removed the pile of refuse. It was then I learned the secret that you have guessed. The refuse was just loaded with maggots of the little brown moth. That was what the bird had been feeding to her young ones, and she never would raise birds on egg food after that. When I could get insects for her she

FEEDING EXPERIMENTS

was all right, but if I could not get them her chicks were sure to die.

Mineral Food Formulae. Ground oyster shell three parts, steamed bone meal one part, salt 1/20th part, sodium phosphate 1/10th part, iodide of potassium ten to twelve grains to each pound. The iodide should be dissolved in water and sprinkled on the dry powder in order to insure a good even mixture. Cuttle bone, hen's egg shell, or ground limestone can be substituted for the oyster shell. One-tenth part of sodium sulphate or 1/20th part of epsom salts may be added to the above.

Color Food. Mix four parts of paprika and one part cayenne pepper, and to each pound of this mixture add three ounces of pure olive oil. This, mixed with the egg food in quantities that will make the food a deep red and fed to moulting birds, will give them a deep color. The petals of most red flowers, fed fresh, will do the same thing. And here it may be remarked that birds enjoy eating most kinds of garden flowers. I have not found any that had an ill effect on the birds. That does not mean that they are all harmless, for I have not tested all flowers by any means.

Tonic Seed and Song Restorers. There are hundreds of mixtures on the market that are supposed to make a bird sing. These are made on the basis of two principles. Tonic seeds are mixtures of the seeds of weeds and flowers that are stimulating to birds and give them certain elements that they need in small quantities to balance their diet and to keep them in health. The mixtures are based upon the assumption that a bird's cravings will tell him more truly what he needs than the breeder could know. A good mixture contains about 20 different kinds of seed, and a given bird eats the ones that he needs and rejects the rest.

Where fed to a large number of birds, some will pick out one seed and some another.

The best tonic seed mixture that I have found contains the following seeds: Niger seed 5 parts, maw seed (blue poppy) 3 parts, whole groat oats 2 parts, mixed red millet 2 parts, flax seed 2 parts, gold of pleasure seed 1 part, grains of paradise seed 1 part, dandelion seed 1 part, white lettuce seed 1 part, sesame seed 1 part, wild weed seeds 3 parts. These weed seeds are cleaned from other seeds and then themselves recleaned by big seed houses. They contain a large number of seeds of weeds of all kinds. The birds like them very much and seem to derive much benefit from them in the tonic mixture. In larger quantities they might not be good.

Treats and song restorers are put up in two ways as well as according to two principles. Some are put up in balls. The seeds and other things are all mixed together and then mixed with sugar, syrup, licorice, or honey, pressed together and baked. The others are put up in boxes, cans, or bottles. The way that the mixture is put up has nothing to do with the principle upon which it is compounded. One set of song-restorers is compounded upon the principle that the average bird owner will put the bird in a fancy round cage, fill its cup with cheap package seed, and then let him starve to death. The mixture is made of good food materials that such a bird would lack in his diet. They contain, besides the tonic seeds, in varying proportions, ground bread, egg, or meat in some form, usually ground rape seed that has been cooked, and a great many of them contain cod liver oil. The others are made up much the same way but contain, in addition to the things mentioned above, drugs that are intended to stimulate the bird or to cure some of his diseases. As there is no way of telling whether the mixture contains drugs or not, it is best to avoid such mixtures unless it is plainly stated on the package that they contain no drugs and are intended as foods only. When your bird needs drugs, give him drugs and know what you are giving him. Never doctor him on general principles, but have some idea of what is wrong with him. Treat him with drugs or medicines that are put up for that special purpose; not with so-called bird tonics that might be all right for some bird that is just run down, but which are not good for your bird at all. The advantage of seed mixtures that contain seed only, as tonics for the run down bird, lies in the fact that you know there is nothing in the mixture that can do him any harm as long as you follow the directions. He gets the food in the natural state, and he is not going to be induced by sweetening to eat something that is not good for him.

CHAPTER V

INSECTS AND PARASITES

MOSQUITOES

During the summer months some breeders notice that certain of their young birds have sores on their feet, or perhaps large clots of blood on their toes; or toes swollen and inflamed. Several birds may have lost the claw or first joint of one or more toes. The disease breaks out about July and continues until November, when it goes away by itself.

These birds are being eaten up, killed, and crippled by mosquitoes. Go into your bird room at night when it is dark with a flash light, sit quietly, and soon if mosquitoes are present, you will hear a peculiar stamping sound from one of the cages. Locating the sound is easy for it is repeated at regular intervals. Flashing on the light quickly, you will see a whole swarm of mosquitoes around the birds' toes. I have seen six on a bird's toe at one time. The bird puffs out his feathers when he goes to sleep and lets them down over his foot to protect all except that one toe, but he has no way to protect that. All he can do is kick at the mosquitoes with his free foot. They fly off and fly right back. The thick scales on an old bird's foot protect it. The best that the mosquito can do is to drill in between the scales, but it can drill right through the scales on a young bird's foot. I have seen young hanging to the perch, head down, dead; and upon examination found their hearts white, every drop of blood

INSECTS AND PARASITES

having been sucked from their bodies by this terrible pest.

To treat mosquito bites anoint the feet of the birds that have sore toes with 1% carbolic vaseline. Screen all windows with 18 mesh wire cloth. Do the same with all out door flights. This will keep out most of the mosquitoes but not all. Make it a habit to spend an hour or so in your darkened bird room every night, and when you hear mosquitoes working, spray Fly-Tox about the room. It is a good idea to do this every evening during the breeding season, for it not only kills any mosquitoes that get in but keeps down lice, mites, and other insects.

LICE AND MITES

If your birds spend much time in scratching themselves, once each week wash all of your cages and equipment in ½% lye solution in hot water or 1% cresol disinfectant in hot soapy water. When you remove a bird to wash his cage, turn him on his back in your hand and spread his wings and tail. If you see any lines on the web of the large feathers extending at right angles from the shaft, you can be sure that your bird has lice.

The adult bird louse lives by sucking the oil from the feathers. It attaches its eggs to the shaft of the large feathers, and when the larvae hatch, they at once begin to eat their way across the web of the feather, always at right angles to the shaft.

These louse-eaten feathers should be pulled out and the bird powdered with a mixture prepared as follows: mix one part of commercial sodium fluoride with four parts of white flour, sift this through a flour sifter several times until it is well mixed, and put some of it in a pepper shaker. This treatment given to the entire flock once each week will keep the birds free from lice under almost any conditions. Every day that the sun shines, I sun my birds under a sparrow roost. Lice are always crawling around on the pavement and brick wall against which I set the cages, but due to this treatment they never bother my birds very much.

Warning: Sodium fluoride is poison. It must not be used in the nests. When cleaning cages always get the litter out of the bird room as quickly as possible. Otherwise lice in the litter will crawl out and right back onto your birds.

MITES

If you have mites in your bird room, follow instructions given for lice, but in addition every night when you cover your birds close the doors and windows of your bird room, spray Fly-Tox until the air appears foggy. Do not shoot it directly on the birds, but if you wish you may create a fog inside the cages without harming them. This is a cheap and easy way to help keep down all insects in the bird room during the breeding season. It will do wonders in that respect, but it will not entirely remove the necessity for using the other methods mentioned.

There are several ways of keeping mites out of the nests. At the beginning of the breeding season cut a number of nest linings from burlap. Dip half of these in cresol disinfectant and let them dry for a few hours. Then in each nest place one of these dipped linings and an undipped lining over it (this keeps the hen from soiling her feathers when she is putting the foundation in the nest). Stack the nests together and place them in a closed can until ready to use. These treated

INSECTS AND PARASITES

linings will get rather dry but they will retain a strong odor of creosote. Before using, the nest should be placed in the air for twenty-four hours. Then after dusting the inside with the sodium fluoride mixture enough nesting should be added to cover it, the nesting being packed down well. Leave the nest for the hen to complete. The odor from the creosote will permeate the nest and make it an unhealthy place for mites, while at the same time being too weak to harm the chicks.

Dusting the inside of the nest with pyrethrum powder is good to keep away lice and mites; also frequent changing of the nests will help. Where a hen for any reason is taken off a nest before it is soiled, the nest should be saved. It should be placed with others in a tall air-tight can that has a handful of mothballs in the bottom of it, and the can should be kept in a warm, but not a hot, place. If the place is too hot the mothballs will be sublimed and deposited all through the nesting material, making the nest unfit for further use, but if the place where the can is kept is not too hot, only the fumes will go into the nesting material and these will evaporate quickly when the nest is taken out and warmed before using. They will have been strong enough, however, to have killed any mites that were in the nest due to its previous use. Such nests can be used as substitutes when there is any suspicion that a nest is infested with mites. If such a change is made the day before the young are due to hatch, little thought need be given to mites for the next ten days. By that time the chicks will be past the danger period.

SCALY LEG MITE

If the feet of your birds always look dirty, examination of them may reveal a growth of thick heavy scales and the feet may be enlarged. The scales will be loose and there will appear to be a white powder under them. This condition is caused by the scaly leg mite, a very small mite that can be seen only under a glass. The white powder is the excreta from the thousands of mites that are eating their way under the scales on the birds' feet and breeding there. This disease usually gets into the bird room with new birds from unclean stock. It spreads very slowly, some birds being immune to attack by this mite; but if not controlled it will eventually spoil the appearance of most of your flock, besides causing your birds a great deal of discomfort.

Fortunately the treatment for this condition is one of the simplest. Anoint the feet of your birds with one percent carbolated vaseline and paint all your perches with cresol disinfectant, thoroughly cleaning them with soap and water. Give the birds a second treatment three days later when all of the infected scales will be loose and can be easily removed. Care should be taken not to make the feet sore. The two treatments are usually enough to stamp out this infection, and it is not likely to return if the perches are kept clean.

FEATHER MITE

Many breeders, when their old birds have lost the feathers on their heads and necks, have been told that the birds are infected with the feather mite. After using a treatment that has not cured the condition, they wonder what can be the cause of the trouble and how to cure it.

Poultry are attacked by a mite which is known as the depluming mite. Several years ago Sub Rosa, writing in *Cage Birds,* London, published a letter from one

INSECTS AND PARASITES 71

of his correspondents reporting a case of depluming mites on a canary suffering with the symptoms of soft moult. Please note: the bird had the symptoms of soft moult, and baldness is not one of those symptoms. The correspondent reported that a single hand washing with Life Buoy Soap was sufficient to cure this infection.

Ever since this article appeared many breeders have gone feather-mite mad. They have smeared up their birds with all kinds of concoctions when the reasons for their trouble were constitutional. (See **Baldness** for a discussion of this condition.)

GAPE

Birds may seem to have something wrong with their throats. Not appearing sick, they fly around, fight and keep their feathers sleek, but they do not seem quite well. They often take naps in the day time, and either when taking a nap or while at rest, every few moments they work their heads as if they had something in their throats and were trying to swallow it or dislodge it.

Birds so afflicted have what is known as gape. They truly have something in their throats: worms in the windpipe. This is a common affliction of baby chicks, often killing them; but it is rather uncommon in canaries. I have seen two cases of it in canaries, have had it in sparrows, have seen quite a few cases of it in wild sparrows, and some in young pigeons. To treat the disease in a bird the size of a sparrow or canary is not easy, because the worms are likely to be so big that they will strangle the bird as they are coming up. A number of treatments are recommended. One is to fish the worms out of the windpipe with a fine wire. I consider this impossible on a canary, although I have read of men claiming to have performed the operation successfully. Another way is to dip a feather in potassium permanganate solution or in turpentine, push it down the windpipe, and then remove it quickly. This will reach some of the worms and give the bird some relief, but I have never been able to get them all with this method. Another treatment is to put into the bird's crop (it will have to be forced down in food) about 1/16 of a grain of santonin. By making the bird gag and vomit this will dislodge some of the worms, but I was not able to get them all out by this method either. The one way of treating this trouble that I have found sure is to introduce a hypodermic needle with a very fine point into the windpipe about half way down. The skin of the bird is so thin that the windpipe is easily seen once the feathers are removed. The bird is wrapped in a piece of bandage to keep him from struggling, the point of the needle is introduced under the skin, and then the windpipe is held firmly and gently between the thumb and forefinger of one hand and the point of the needle worked in between two of the rings. About one-tenth of a drop of one percent solution of potassium permanganate is injected, the needle removed quickly, and the bird released at once. He will gag, kick, struggle, and gasp. If the worms are too big for him to get up, he may choke to death; but a bird does not choke so easily as one might think, and if the worms can be worked out he will be cured. Care, however, must be taken to see that he does not get reinfected.

This trouble comes from giving the birds sand or green food taken from the neighborhood of a poultry yard or sparrow roost. The eggs of these worms are passed out by the millions in the droppings of infected birds. When taken into the body of a well bird they

INSECTS AND PARASITES

soon hatch out, and the young worm makes its way at once to the wind pipe. To avoid reinfection the equipment should be thoroughly cleaned and disinfected, and care taken to see that infected material is not thereafter given to the birds.

There are many other parasitic infections that sometimes may be encountered in a canary, but most of them are uncommon and when found are undoubtedly due to keeping birds in filthy surroundings or to introducing into your flock birds that have not been properly cared for. It is a good plan never to place a new bird with your flock until you are sure that he is absolutely healthy.

CHAPTER VI

THE MOULT

THE PHYSIOLOGY OF THE MOULT

Many breeders look upon the moult as a thing to be dreaded and it is indeed true that birds are out of condition at that time. They have special needs that must be cared for; they will stop singing, become sick, and even die if these needs are neglected; but the well treated bird will sing every day of his moult and give his owner not one moment of worry. He must have the food out of which to make feathers and must have correct temperatures.

Growth of body, growth of feathers, and the growth of eggs as well as other bodily functions are controlled by the so-called "ductless glands." These are in turn influenced by external conditions and by the food supply. When the thyroid gland is over active (and this activity is communicated to the sex glands) we have the bird in breeding condition. A reduction of the activity of the thyroid gland gives us a sluggish bird that puts on fat and cannot be made to breed. When it becomes still less active, or its activity is of a different nature, the bird goes into moult. If the balance is correct the bird will grow a complete set of feathers and then stop moulting, but if the balance is upset the bird will stop moulting without growing a complete set of feathers, or it will go into soft moult and possibly continue to grow feathers until it moults itself to death.

THE MOULT

When a moulting bird is placed on a breeding diet, placed in a cooler room, chilled, or shocked in any way, it is likely to stop moulting before the growth of feathers has been completed. When this happens nine breeders out of ten become excited believing that so-called feather mites are involved.

That the moult may be controlled through the influence of temperature has long been known and been made use of by many breeders, although it still seems not to be understood by a great many. It is often too troublesome to be of value to the breeders who do understand it; so many breeders have tried to control the moult by the use of drugs. Potassium chlorate and cod liver oil have been of some value in causing moult, and citrate of iron and quinine is valuable in stopping the moult. There are many cases where both the heat control and drugs fail to bring about the desired results, and in the hope of finding a better method I undertook some experiments with the use of gland products. The experiments are not complete, but it has been found that thyroid extract will stop soft moult and cause the reduction of fat on overfat birds thus bringing them into breeding condition. This extract comes in one grain tablets for human use and for a canary should be diluted with 100 parts of sugar; the bird is then given ½ grain of the dilution in some soft food of which it is fond every day for from three to five days. This is a dangerous drug and must not be used for too long a time or without regard to its reaction. When the bird begins to breathe fast and becomes nervous, it is time to discontinue the drug, and I do not think that in any case it is necessary to use it for a whole week or that this can be done without danger.

For the opposite effect thyroid residue is used. This is what is left after the nucleo-protein has been extracted from the thyroid glands of cattle and sheep. It is purchasable as a liquid and contains about 5% of organically combined iodine. For birds stuck in moult (that is, bald birds) the drug is used in a dilution of 1 to 20, and the dose is one to three drops to the ounce of drinking water. This may be used somewhat longer than the extract, and the reaction is just the opposite from that of the extract. The bird breathes more slowly, becomes sluggish, and goes into moult. But as I said above, the experiments have not been completed and I am not able to say that either of these methods is safe or practical. They are offered here as a suggestion for experimental work by others and I shall continue them myself. This is a new and interesting field and one that holds promise of providing us with methods of considerable importance; direct control of the physiological factors involved.'

INDIGESTION DUE TO IMPROPER FEEDING DURING MOULT

Frequently a canary, kept as a pet by its owner who is not a breeder, will finish his moult with a full coat of feathers but will not resume his song. He is

---

[3]In many species of birds, temperature is, I believe, not a factor at all. I have had Baltimore orioles, indigo bunting, orchard orioles moult indoors in December, January and February at the time when their comrades that had migrated to the tropics were, presumably, passing through the same condition. At least they return with changed plumage. Birds from below the equator moult at a time when they would moult in their native habitat, lay their eggs then, etc. which seems to point to periodicity rather than temperature in such cases, canaries and hens to the contrary notwithstanding. On the other hand experiments have been made in Germany with nightingales under the influence of temperature and moisture which has postponed or hastened the moult and thus kept birds of this species in song all the year round. Ordinarily their song lasts only for May and June. (Editor's Note.)

THE MOULT

very light in weight, seems always hungry, but often stops eating and sits with his eyes closed. His droppings are soft and watery.

This condition is caused by trying to moult a bird without giving him the food to make feathers. Many owners of pet birds are too stupid to realize that they cannot get something for nothing when they buy package seed of the cheapest grade; and that their birds cannot get something from nothing when they try to make a coat of feathers on a diet of that kind. Seed, even if it is of the best, cannot give the bird all the elements that he needs to make a coat of feathers in the proportion in which he needs them. To get salts and vitamins that he needs he has to consume many times the amount of seed he would otherwise eat, and the strain at last is too much for even a bird's wonderful digestion.

This trouble can be avoided by feeding the bird as he should be fed during the moult. See that the moulting bird gets rape and canary, more canary than rape in the mixture, in his seed cup and that it is the very best grade of fresh clean seed. See that he has some vitamin D every day or two, together with all the green food that he can eat, and if possible, plenty of fresh seeding grasses. Give him a little sod once in a while, a little egg-food daily, and mix some tonic seeds into the egg-food. See that he has plenty of cuttle bone or other mineral food. Keep him from getting chilled, and he will sing every day of his moult. Many persons have the idea that it is necessary for birds to stop singing during moult, but the well treated bird never does. He may sing a little less than usual, but most of my birds sing all day long during moult, and when one stops I know that I have neglected him in some way and attend to it at once.

The bird that is already suffering with this indigestion and is sick should receive the care just described, and he must have plenty of exercise, too, to help rebuild his body. Even these things will not always save him, for germs attack his inflamed digestive tract and he goes from bad to worse. Such birds have an abnormal thirst. No food will agree with them, and they will empty their drinking cups within a few hours. This condition can best be treated by mixing Stroud's Avian Antiseptic and Stroud's Effervescent Salts in equal parts and putting from $\frac{1}{2}$ to 1 grain in each ounce of drinking water; at the same time feeding as directed above and giving plenty of sod with clean, black loam earth around its roots. As soon as the bird's bowels become normal, the medical treatment should be discontinued. If this treatment is not available, fairly good results can be had by putting a little peroxide of hydrogen in the drinking water along with some citrocarbonate. Mix one part of citric acid with two parts by weight of bicarbonate of soda to form a wet paste. Dry it and powder it. Since this is very light in weight, a pile about the size of a pea is only about one-half grain and is the right amount for a one-ounce drinker. To this add ten drops of commercial peroxide of hydrogen solution to the ounce of water. This treatment should be given only until the bowels clear up. Never under any circumstances overdose a bird.

BALDNESS

Out of all the letters reaching me probably more contain requests for advice on baldness than on any other ailment to which a bird is subject. I say "ailment" for in most cases the loss of feathers is due to some factor upsetting the normal physiological function of the moult. There are a great many things that can do this. Wrong diet, wrong management, over-breeding all help to swell the number of birds with featherless heads and necks; wrong advice put out by those who should know better, even if they do not, does not decrease the number.

The Moult

Before we can understand just why a bird does not have the feathers that nature intended, it is necessary for us to understand something of nature's process by which the normal bird is supplied with its feathers. Nature has provided that a bird shall grow one coat of feathers each year. In the wild state this takes place in our latitude and in the northern hemisphere in the latter part of July, in August, and the first part of September. The moult begins at the hottest period of the year and ends at the time when the first cool weather of autumn may be expected. These facts should be kept in mind for they furnish us with the only reliable means of controlling the moult that is now known.

When a bird is placed in a room having an abnormally high temperature, or when he is subjected to sudden variations in temperature he will almost always go into the moult. The temperature changes appear to upset the functioning of the thyroid gland which governs to some extent all growth activities, although there are other glands that play an equally important part. Really it is a balance between the activities of a number of glands that govern the state of the body. And in this question of feathers the sex glands are of primary importance. When the sex glands are active the **bird does not** moult. The male will be in full song and the female will be in breeding condition. They will both be very active and have a high rate of metabolism (the process by which food is converted into energy).

When the sex glands are active there is also increased activity in the thyroid gland. When the thyroid gland is inactive the bird cannot be brought into breeding condition, will be sluggish, inactive and will put on fat with great ease. Males and females alike will sit around with the feathers held loosely. They are not sick; but the males will not sing and the females will not mate. They go into moult easily when placed in a room having too high a temperature. This last state corresponds to the winter condition of birds in the wild state. It is a natural provision whereby the body decreases its activities during the months of bad weather and stores up fuel as a protection against interrupted food supply. The loosely carried feathers enable the bird to keep itself warm with the expenditure of the least amount of energy, and every grain of fat that it carries may be needed to sustain life should it be caught in a blizzard.

Now it is a commonly observed fact that where two physiological functions depend upon each other as cause and effect, the existence of either will tend to bring about the existence of the other. The existence of the moult will stop breeding, the existence of too much fat will also stop breeding, while stimulation of the sex glands will stop moulting and lead to the reduction of fat. While birds live in the natural state the bodily functions fall into a natural order, but when man takes a hand this order is very often upset and it becomes impossible to say which comes first. It is like the classical problem of the chicken or the egg. This will be better

THE MOULT

understood in connection with the actual causes of upset moult that will presently be given.

Kinds of Baldness

There are five kinds of baldness known in canaries. They are:

(1) **Congenital Baldness.** There are two ways this may be brought about. When two crested birds are bred together they often throw chicks having deformed head featherings. Some of these chicks may have great masses of feathers on their head while others may have bald spots. Such bald spots are present from the time that the bird hatches. They never have had any feathers or even fuzz on them. When a crested bird is mated to birds having no crested blood and this is carried on over several generations the crest becomes smaller with each generation and will develop defects, such as clefts of naked spots in the center. A continuation of such breeding methods may lead to birds that are totally bald on the tops of their heads. In this case there must be crested blood, and crested birds. It matters not whether inbreeding or outbreeding leads to the baldness; it is in every case a defective crest that we see when we look at the bald head. Only the head is affected.

The second way in which baldness can be brought about by breeding is where two yellow birds are mated together. I use the term "yellow" here in its technical sense, meaning a bird that has the color extended uniformly throughout the web of the feathers, as distinguished from the buff bird that has a colorless edging around the web of each feather. When two yellow birds are mated together the feathers become thinner, narrower, harder, more brittle and shorter. This does not happen in the wild state for the simple reason that in the wild state the canary is dark green with almost no trace of yellow except here and there yellowish green. The yellow canary is an albino like the yellow parrakeets that are also not found wild. Where this line of breeding is continued for some years the feathers become so short and brittle that the birds will seem to be half naked most of the time.

For congenital baldness there is no cure. If the crested bird that is bald is of value, it may be bred to a crest bred bird with good head feathers and will produce some normal young. If the short feathered yellow bird is of value it may be bred to a heavily feathered buff bird and produce normal feathers.

(2) **Baldness Due to Upset Moult.** Roller breeders often have this in their young males. Most young males are changed to the singing cages at the time they are feathering their heads at the end of the baby moult. Some of them are apt to be well advanced in their song and the breeder is over anxious to get them into the singing cages and on to a song diet before they develop faults that will make them worthless as show birds. The birds are transferred a little too soon and the diet changed a little too drastically. The result is that the bird comes into full song almost at once and at the same time stops moulting the head feathers. The baby feathers that are still on the head and neck will not stand the wear placed upon them. They soon wear out and the bird is bald. This same thing may happen with any moulting bird. A cold room, a too stimulating diet that brings the bird into breeding condition before the moult is ended, may stop the bird from moulting all of its feathers and then if a new moult is not forced the bird will go bald.

THE MOULT

(3) **Baldness Due to Exhaustion.** This is a modification of the case described above, though more serious. Many breeders, especially the novices, will overfeed their hens at the end of the breeding season. They may want that extra nest of birds or they may merely be ignorant and think that they are being kind to their birds. The over-fed hen stays in breeding condition. Often it happens that she has started to moult while raising a nest of birds and has been stimulated in order to save the birds. Often she has been bred for five, six, or even eight nests with no regard to her condition. She does not moult, the feathers that she has wear out, and she is left naked. In many cases she has been so exhausted that should she be forced into a moult she will die, because she is unable to metabolize the materials necessary for the production of feathers.

(4) **Baldness Due to Lack of the Food Necessary for Feather Production.** Many persons who keep singers do not realize that a bird needs special food during the moulting season and do not give the bird the food necessary to make the feathers. They feed him on some stale package seed and discolored lettuce leaves and expect him to grow a coat of feathers on that. Well he usually tries and makes a fair job of it, but he ruins his digestion in the process, and is very apt to die just about the time he gets nicely feathered. But in some cases he saves his digestion and goes bald.

(5) **Baldness Due to the Loss or Destruction of Feathers.** Birds normally grow but one coat of body feathers per year. If the large feathers are pulled out or damaged they will be replaced at anytime, for nature has been wise enough to provide against the loss of flight power (which would mean the loss of life in the

wild state) which would follow if a bird could not replace its flight feathers at any time; but the body feathers, and often the tail feathers, once lost, are not as a rule replaced until the next moult.

The body feathers may be lost by hand washing a bird and removing all the oil from the feathers and then not removing all the soap. The feathers become dry and brittle and soon the bird is bald. They may be lost by fighting, feather plucking, or excessive lice and mite infection. And I believe that they may be lost because of *feather mites*. There are those who would have us believe that every case of baldness is due to feather mites. Possibly I am not a close observer, but, frankly, I have never seen a case of baldness due to this cause and doubt very much whether those who report this have actually ever seen such a case or could tell what a feather mite looks like. How many anterior claws has it and how many posterior horns or hairs? This does not mean that I doubt the existence of a depluming mite. It is a common infection of poultry and pigeons and is very closely related to the scaly leg mite. They look very much alike but the feather mite is only about half as large as the scaly leg mite, that is, about 1/100 of an inch long, exclusive of projecting processes, and the feather mite about 1/200 of an inch long exclusive of projecting processes. Neither of them causes much trouble in canaries and both are easily exterminated by a very simple means which I have described elsewhere.

Treatment of Baldness

(1) There is no treatment of congenital baldness that can ever be effective. It would be as impossible to make such a bird grow feathers on skin having no

THE MOULT

feather follicle as it would be to make a man grow three legs or an extra ear or nose.

(2) It is only necessary to remoult birds that have become bald because of interrupted moult. This can be done by placing the birds in a very warm place as a rule, or by moving them from place to place daily for several weeks. I think that it is usually the best plan to treat the bird so as to keep it in perfect health and wait for the next moult to correct its appearance.

(3) The case of the bird exhausted from over breeding is not so simple. It is often impossible to force such birds into moult by the usual processes, and I have found that the best method is to turn such birds into flight for six months or more and then, if they do not remoult themselves, to try to cause them to remoult. It is useless to try to breed such birds, for in that condition they cannot produce chicks that will live, though once they have gotten to moult fully they are as good as they ever were. I have been experimenting on the action of thyroid gland products in the control of this condition. There is a drug produced from the thyroid glands of cattle and sheep that is known as Thyroid Residue. It comes in liquid form and must be diluted with water and alcohol in equal parts in the ratio of one part of the drug to twenty parts of the solvent before using it on a canary. The dose of this one to twenty solution is one to three drops to the ounce of drinking water. Its physiological effect is to decrease the activity of the thyroid gland and the sex gland. My experiments with this drug are incomplete, so that I cannot say just how valuable it will prove in this respect.

(4) The only thing to do in cases where a bird has not had the necessary food is first to build up the health of the bird and then cause it to remoult.

(5) The only sensible treatment of a bird that has lost any or all of its feathers from some external cause is to remove the cause and then wait for the next moult to correct the bird's appearance. Dosing the bird with dangerous drugs (most of the drugs sold for this purpose are preparations of potassium chlorate) or dabbing it with blisters (the salves sold for this purpose are mostly blisters made from carbolic acid and vaseline, or sulphur) is needless cruelty. Blistering the skin will in some cases make the feathers grow on the blistered part, but when a bird has lost enough feathers to make it bald the use of a blister over the entire area would probably kill the bird.

The Moulting of Breeding Stock

Almost every breeder has some birds that fall into moult and then stop at the end of the breeding season. Some of these birds will later be unable to complete the moult; they will continue in breeding condition until they exhaust themselves and are ruined. This condition is due to failure on the part of the breeder to follow the correct routine at the end of the breeding season. For the benefit of breeders having this moulting trouble in their flocks I will describe a system that I have found to work very well.

When I get ready to discontinue breeding, four flights, each large enough to hold from 16 to 20 birds, are made ready. Two of these flights are so arranged that they can be darkened at any time of the day. As

THE MOULT

the hen comes into condition, she is taken away, and the cock left to wean the last nest of birds alone. The hen is placed at once in one of these flights. The food is cut down at once to canary and rape in the seed cups, with green food and cuttle bone as the only extras. These birds are not given the light until 8:00 or 9:00 o'clock in the morning; they are put to bed at 2:00, 3:00, or 4:00 o'clock in the afternoon. During the middle of the day they are given a bath in the direct sunshine.

When the males finish weaning the chicks, they are put into the other darkening flight and given the same treatment except that I have found it best to give them a little tonic seed and a little egg food every day. About one ounce egg cup full of the two mixed together for each ten birds is enough.

Once each week the cages are washed and sterilized, as are all my cages, and at this time every one of these birds is inspected closely. I note the amount of weight lost and the growth of new feathers. As soon as each bird is moulting well, and the abdomen has lost its fat, it is placed in the second flight, males in one, females in another. In this second flight the amount of egg food and tonic seed is increased two or three times and the eating day lengthened in order to keep the birds in good condition and provide them with the necessary food elements to make their new coat; but great caution is exercised in order to see that no bird is too greatly reduced on the one hand and that none come back into breeding condition on the other. Any hen that goes into a very violent moult and is evidently not getting enough food in this second flight to carry her over is put into the young hens' flight. Any hen that exhibits signs of breeding condition while in flight number two is put back into flight number one at once. The same treatment is given to the cocks. None of the cocks is returned to the singing cages until the moult is over.

By the use of the method for the last two years I have had but one hen "stuck in moult" and have not had a single male stop singing during the moult or fail to feather perfectly. Not one bird has been lost during moult in that time. As the males complete their moult they are returned to the singing cages and as the females, both old and young, complete the moult they are put into their winter flight and provided with their winter diet, which is seed, green food, and egg with tonic seed twice each week. The eating day of the females is limited to about 7 or 8 hours out of the 24 during the entire winter. Hens wintered by this method do not come into breeding condition in January. Some of them may not be ready to breed until April; but when they are ready, there are few dead babies in the nests, for the hens are in perfect condition themselves and can produce perfect chicks and give them perfect care. One infrequent cause of baldness in canaries, which may be mentioned here for the sake of completeness, is a skin disease due to infection with a pathogenic mould (fungus) that is very closely related to ring-worm in human beings. This condition is discussed fully elsewhere in this book.

CHAPTER VII

INJURIES AND ACCIDENTS

Broken Bones in General

Fractures may be divided into three classes: when the bones are broken but the ends are not separated, as commonly occurs in the case of nestling canaries but which is often met with in old birds too, we have what is called a "simple fracture"; those where the bones are separated without a rupture of the skin I shall refer to as "aggravated fractures"; those in which the bone sticks out through the skin are referred to as "compound fractures". In the treatment of simple fractures it is only necessary to place the limb in such a position that the bone is straight and remains so during healing. In the case of an aggravated fracture it is first necessary to set the bone so that the ends come together and then provide some method of holding it in that position until the bone heals. In compound fractures it is also necessary to dress the wound that the bone has made where it passed through the skin. This is very difficult and it is usually the best method to kill the bird that has suffered a compound fracture; although there are a few cases that can be treated successfully.

Broken Wings

Simple fractures of the wings are the most common of all fractures suffered by old birds. It is usually the humerus bone that is broken, but sometimes it may be the radius or ulna. This usually happens when the bird is struggling to keep from being caught or held. The first thing noticed is that when the bird is replaced in the cage it cannot fly and droops one wing. If the wing droops down in a natural line, the breeder can be sure that the fracture is a simple one and he should repress any desire to examine it. For any attempt either to examine or set a simple wing fracture is almost certain to aggravate the injury and lead to a crippled bird. The correct treatment is to place the bird in a cage having all but the lower perches removed. Some advise that all perches should be removed, but I find that this is not necessary. The bird can hop up on the low perch without using its wings, and it will rest more comfortably on the perch and make less effort to fly about. The cage should be placed in a quiet, secluded corner where there is no danger of the bird's being frightened. Food and water should be placed within easy reach and the bird left to itself. The bird will droop the upper part of the wing the correct amount necessary to hold the bone straight, and the wing will heal perfectly in ten days. The bird will be just as good as it ever was.

Sometimes it will be noticed that the lower part of the drooped wing makes an unnatural angle with the upper part. When this is seen, you can be sure that the fracture is an aggravated one. The bird should be caught and the wing set.

To set an aggravated fracture of the wing so that the bird will not be crippled is very difficult, but if care is used the fracture can be set well enough for the bird to be able to fly after it is healed. Proceed as follows: cut two strips of adhesive tape about 1/8 of an inch wide and long enough to pass one and a half times around the bird's body. At the same time two strips of thin paper should be cut the same width as the tape

INJURIES AND ACCIDENTS

but not quite long enough to reach around the body. The tape is warmed and the paper stuck to the gummed side, leaving ½ inch of exposed gum on one end of the tape and about 1½ inches of exposed gum on the other end.

With the tapes ready the bird is caught and while it is held firmly in one hand with the uninjured wing against the palm of the hand and the injured wing held in place by the fingers, the tip of the forefinger is slipped under the injured wing, and, working by the sense of touch, and with the aid of the thumb, the break is located and the bones worked into place so that the two broken ends are in contact. In some cases the wing once set will stay in position. To learn whether it will do so, place the bird on the bottom of a small singing cage for a moment. If he holds the wing in line nothing more is necessary except to treat him as already described.

If, when the bird is placed on the bottom of the singing cage, the wing again bends out at an unnatural angle, the work is to be repeated; and when the bones are again in position the end of the tape having the short gummed portion exposed is stuck to the injured wing. It should be stuck firmly to the large feathers. The tape is then passed around the body and pulled up rather tightly and lapped on itself. This prevents gumming up the feathers.

The second piece of tape should be stuck to the forward angle of the wing (this corresponds to the wrist joint in a human being) and carried around the body just about the uninjured wing. The tape is lapped as before. If the job has been done well, the bird will be able to fly when the tape is taken off ten days later, but the wing will almost always be carried in an unnatural position and the flight will not be so good as before the injury.

Another common injury of the wing is the dislocation of the wrist joint (the joint between the metacarpus and carpus bones on the one hand and the radius and ulna on the other). This joint has to carry the full force of the large flight feathers. The bones are bound together with heavy bands of ligament. Once these are ruptured, they do not heal easily. I have kept birds with their wings bound to the body for over one month but have never known a case of a dislocation of this joint to heal sufficiently to support flight. The best policy is to kill the bird at once.

And right here let me digress long enough to state that the most humane way to kill a bird is not to waste time getting your neighbor or the druggist to chloroform it. Take the bird in your hand with the back toward your thumb and the head extending out over your forefinger. Place the tip of the thumb at the base of the skull, bring the forefinger up under the beak and force the head sharply back until the neck is broken. It takes but a fraction of a second and the bird dies quickly and practically painlessly. The pressure is maintained for a moment during the death spasm.

Broken Legs

The metatarsus bone (the unfeathered leg) of the foot and the tibia (the first bone of the true feathered leg) are the ones usually broken.

Most fractures of the metatarsus are simple because the ligaments and the heavy scaly skin tend to hold the bone in place. Practically all fractures of the tibia are aggravated.

In setting fractures of the metatarsus the best method that I have found is to cut a strip of rather stiff

INJURIES AND ACCIDENTS

paper as wide as the bone is long and about 3/4 of an inch long. Wind this first about a nail the size of the leg to form it into a tube. Partly unroll it and paint the outer end with hot stiff wood glue. Wind this snugly around the leg and hold it till the glue sets. If it is an old bird, the paper should be covered with adhesive tape to keep the bird from taking it off. If it is a nestling no covering is necessary. It is inadvisable to bind the leg with thread. If this is done one is almost sure to cut off the blood supply and the foot will wither very quickly. Never remove the perches from the cage when a bird has a broken leg. He can stand on a perch with one foot but he cannot stand on the cage bottom with the one.

Many young birds will have this bone broken during banding. After the birds are banded their legs should be inspected, and if any are broken they should be set at once. A young bird's bones are growing. They are soft and they bend and break easily. If set at once they will heal as easily and without any permanent injury to the bird, but if neglected for a single day it may be difficult to set them properly.

Where a break is located above the ankle joint on the feathered part of the leg, it is not quite so easy to set. I have never been able to set a break in this part of the leg with splints, although I have heard of others doing it. Such breaks can be set in casts, however. The cast may be made from plaster of Paris, water-glass (sodium silicate), or stiff wood glue. The most satisfactory method that I have found is to wrap a little cotton around the leg, apply the hot glue so stiff that it will set quickly, and hold the leg in place until the glue does set. A paper tube can also be used.

Young birds often suffer leg and foot injuries in the nest due to too much handling or to the nest not being correctly shaped to protect them from the weight of the hen.⁶ Chasing the hen from the nest to look at the chicks is one way to increase the proportion of such injuries. Changing nests is another.

The commonest injury of the foot is due to a misshaped nest and is known as "slipped claw." The back claw turns up between the front toes, and it is impossible for the bird to grasp the perch. There are those who give out the misinformation that this deformity is due to inbreeding. This is untrue. It is a simple case of nest injury. It happens very often when the hen has only one or two chicks and can usually be avoided by leaving in clear eggs or a nest egg in all short nests. Usually a slipped claw is not discovered until the young leave the nest. This can be avoided, however, if the breeder, when inspecting his birds, will make it a practice to tap the nest so that they all rise up to be fed, and then looking at their legs and feet to notice whether they stand normally. If they remain down in the nest and do not attempt to stand while being fed, it is a fairly certain sign that they have been injured.

To treat a slipped claw it is only necessary to fasten the claw back against the metatarsus until it has had time to grow into place. This will take from one week to one month, depending on the age of the bird. I have cured such cases after the bird was a year old. Often the joint will be swollen and the back side

---

⁶"I have always thought this to be, at least in some cases, incipient or arrested rickets. I have had it in native birds that had never been in any nest but their own and then not so long as usual, and I have cured it by the use of Super D cod liver oil in small doses. I believe at least it disappeared on the use of Super D. cod liver oil. (Editor's Note.)

INJURIES AND ACCIDENTS

of the claw calloused so that the claw cannot be placed back against the leg at once without breaking it. In such cases the claw should be forced back as far as possible and kept there for a week and then rebandaged. Some recommend a small section of rubber tubing for this purpose. I have found ordinary adhesive tape satisfactory.

Egg Rupture

The canary breeder is often asked what the result will be in the event a hen breaks an egg inside her abdomen. The general answer is that she will die at once. This answer is not based upon actual experience, however, for very few breeders have ever seen a hen with a ruptured egg. Fragile as the egg may seem to be, it has a surprising resistance to injury while held under the evenly distributed pressure of the oviduct. In all of my years of breeding I have seen just two cases where an egg was broken inside of the hen. In the first case the bird fell thirteen feet to a cement floor while fighting. The egg was ruptured and the bird died 48 hours later of peritonitis. In the other case the egg was ruptured in the lower part of the oviduct. The accident was not observed. The hen was in a large flight and she was noticed several times during the day to be showing signs of distress. The feathers were held loosely and she was breathing too fast, but still eating and drinking. Looking up at her while she was standing on a perch, I noticed that she was straining and that the vent was inflamed. A towel was tossed over her in order to catch her without any risk of injury.

Upon inspection considerable inflammation of the abdomen was noted, and right above the vent on the left side was a hard misshapen lump. I thought that it was a case of inflammation of the oviduct, not suspecting that it was a broken egg. A blunt glass syringe was passed into the vent and about six drops of antiseptic solution injected. The bird was placed on a perch in a small cage. In two minutes she passed the broken egg. The moment she was relieved of the egg her actions became normal and there were no after effects.

Prolapse of the Uterus

This is a rare condition in canaries caused from injuries suffered during the passage of the eggs. It is very rare except in birds that have been greatly weakened by over breeding. The organ protrudes from the vent and is seen as a highly congested mass of dark red tissue. If discovered at once the organ can be forced back into the vent and a few drops of cold salt water injected. This will cause the tissues to contract and remain in place.

Usually the hen will have picked at the protruding part and seriously injured it before the breeder discovers her plight. Where the injury has been extensive, the best thing to do is to kill the bird, for there is little chance of her ever being of any value. If the injury has not been too extensive, the part may be forced back and a strong solution of Avian Antiseptic injected into the cloaca (the sac-like expansion just inside the vent). Sometimes the bird will recover. Needless to say, though, such a bird should not be mated again soon. She should be put in flight until the next season.

CHAPTER VIII

SEPTIC FEVER

General Discussion

I have been fighting this scourge for about four or five months.[1] It has caused the loss of over fifty birds and an economic loss that would be conservatively estimated at $500.00, not to mention labor and worry. That such losses would be serious to anyone is easily understood, but to any one whose birds are his only resource, they are doubly so. It is, however, not this part of the subject I wish to discuss.

It is quite true that the source of the trouble is in imported birds. For years I have bought a dozen or so imported birds, direct from the importers, every winter. I have never found a case of septic fever in the early importations, but I have never found a shipment after the holidays that did not contain one or more cases. These were expected and dealt with. Birds were all placed in singing cages and closely observed for two weeks, and every bird which exhibited the symptoms was killed. The disease, therefore, never got beyond control. I think perhaps the reason the disease is more prevalent after the holidays is that during the holiday rush the same equipment is used again and again without any attempt to sterilize it.

Last winter I had need of some particular birds. They had to have certain feather qualities, as well as certain song qualities. After a search in Kansas City

---

[1]The first part of this chapter contains the announcement of the discovery of a treatment for the cure of septic fever. With a few changes it is the same discussion of this subject that appeared in *The Roller Canary Journal and Bird World* of September, 1928.

and its vicinity, I had failed to locate what I needed. I got in touch with a *Journal* advertiser who handles large quantities of domestic as well as imported birds and who boasts of his perfect sanitation. He said he could supply my needs. I paid his highest price, which was considerably more than the importer's price, and closed my order with these words: "I assume that birds are guaranteed free from contagion. If you are not absolutely certain on this point, do not ship." The search I had made for the birds I required had taken time. It was late in the season, and I had twelve pairs mated. The birds came; they were good birds in excellent condition with the exception of one hen and one male that were out of order; I believed this due to exposure in shipment. There was no symptom of contagion but they were killed and the rest quarantined for ten days. They seemed to be in excellent condition. A cock and two hens were mated, he being given half a day with each. When he was removed from the cage of the last hen so that she could complete her clutch, a sore on his ear was noticed. It was four days later before the sore spread and the general symptoms developed. He was killed. Both hens developed the disease, the first symptoms being noted the day before birds were due to hatch. One was killed, but the other, whose cage was at the end of the row where she would not be apt to endanger others, was treated and studied. Each sore was opened and burned out with saturated solution of potassium permanganate. The dissections and symptomatic study had convinced me that the disease was analagous to roup in chickens, and diphtheria in human beings. I addressed my treatment to the removal of the toxins from the blood, on the theory applied to the treatment of diphtheria before the development of antitoxins, that is, by the use of saline

SEPTIC FEVER

laxatives and diuretics. This took no account of the bowel condition. I further ignored it by feeding all the green food the bird would eat, and she ate great quantities of it and little else. She got well. She was later killed and dissected; was full of eggs and all organs normal. The five eggs from the other hen were given to an old hen who was a good feeder but of no particular value inasmuch as her breeding days were over. The eggs were dipped in germicide before transfer. All hatched and four lived. Two of the four developed the disease on the 28th day and the other two not until ten days later. It was still later that the hen developed the disease and was promptly killed.

That there had been, up until this time, no general outbreak was no doubt due to my system. Some years ago I had trouble with lice. Now, every bird gets powdered and inspected once a week, and every cage washed in strong disinfectant once a week. Bath houses are all numbered and cups are all thoroughly disinfected. The general outbreak came, however, and it raked my breeding cages from end to end. My chart is filled with notations—"a hen and three chicks—fever," "hen, cock, and five chicks—fever." But here is a point of interest: my cocks in the singing cages were all carried into the sunshine for 1½ hours daily. The same is true of my hens in flight. Not one case developed in either of these groups. My best birds were given to my mother, one or two at a time, and kept in quarantine for one month by her. This enabled me to have enough left, so as not to be obliged to start again from the beginning, but even so, some of the best were lost.

After using the "kill and disinfect" method for over a month, (in one week of which I killed twenty-one birds), I was rather disgusted. I did not expect to save any, and was on the point of killing the lot, to end the worry. I, however, changed my mind and dedicated the birds to experimentation and search for a specific. I had studied the disease closely. I could detect it before the onset of the malignant stage which precedes death and which is usually the first sign noted. I established these facts: that the period of incubation of the germ lasts from eight to twenty-one days (there was only one case of eight days, all the others taking fourteen or more); that it is only in the last three or four days of the incubation period that disease can be transmitted to another bird; that from the end of the incubation period until malignant state is reached it may take from four to ten days. and from the beginning of the last active stage until death may be from four to nine days. The end of the period of incubation is detected by a slight change in the color of droppings; by a slightly increased rate of breathing; or by a minute blister on some part of the body—usually on the head or vent, but perhaps on the foot or wing. Any one of these indications may be present without the other. These birds appear young, and carry on every normal function. Disease may be arrested so that the following stage takes on a mild form. The bowel action clears up in about ten days, and if the sore does not spread there is no fever. A bird in this condition will breed and raise chicks, but will infect any bird with which it comes in contact. I have one such hen that raised her nest, infected the male, and is now raising a second nest. The only indication is a tiny blister on her head, not so big as the head of a pin. It would be very hard to see if feathers were not picked off, and it is hardly visible even with the feathers removed. It discharges constantly, however, a transparent liquid that is no doubt the source of the spread of the disease. I have also found that in the absence of any treatment, infection upon contact is 100 per cent, but if a saline laxative and diuretic, such as those prepared for human use, is given, one teaspoonful to the quart of water, the percentage of cases developed falls off to less than 25 per cent of the birds exposed by direct contact. I believe that the removal of seed and green food is a mistake. Birds will eat little seed but crave green food. We crave what we need. An infected sparrow will eat only green food and black loam dirt, and he will recover.

As I said, I was looking for a specific. The experiments and reasoning I followed would take too long to recite but were based upon some personal experience with diphtheria in human beings, the idea being to find something that would kill the germ and not kill the bird. I believe I have found that something. One bird, not over twenty-four hours from death, was singing in forty-eight hours, and entirely well in nine days. Three early-treated young males never stopped their song study. Two were completely cured; one seems to be in chronic stage. This substance is a powerful commercial germicide but is non-poisonous to birds, and will not even hurt a day-old chick.[8]

It is in the first part of the year that many breeders blast their own hopes for the breeding season and suffer serious losses in their flocks, if not the loss of their entire flocks, by buying birds that are infected with this dreaded disease. Therefore a few more words

---

[8]At the time the above was written there was much that I did not know about this disease, but the observations were fresh in my mind. It was these same observations, along with the discussions of this disease by other writers at about this time, that were responsible for my taking up the scientific study of the diseases of canaries. What follows was written for the *Journal*, January, 1932, and gives a fuller treatment of this disease.

on this all-important subject are now timely. Imported birds are being brought into the country in large numbers. Due to the depressed conditions in Europe, especially in England and Germany, breeders there are being forced to sacrifice their best birds for a song. The result is that the birds now being brought in are better than ever before, and they are selling at the lowest price in many years. It is not to be wondered at that many breeders are tempted to add to their stock birds that appear to be exceptional bargains. They do not realize that at this season every bird that passes through our importing and jobbing houses is exposed to this highly contagious disease.

In the cities, many stores are having bird sales. They advertise a bird in a cage at a price as low as two dollars. They tell you that many of the birds are singers, but they are not guaranteed to be and cannot be exchanged at that price. I had a friend visit one of these bird sales for me. There were fifty birds on display. Questioning of the clerk revealed that the birds came from the same jobbing house from which I buy sick birds for experimental purposes. These culls are worth about $6.00 per dozen from the jobbers. They contain cull hens that have poor feathers or something else wrong with them and the birds that arrive sick in the shipments of imported males. So the statement is true that some are males. In the lot under discussion there were at most about five males and everyone of them was near death with the fever, though one not knowing this disease would not have realized it. Of the whole lot there was only one bird that did not show the sulphur colored droppings characteristic of this disease. My friend arrived at the store a short time before the sale was scheduled to commence. None of the birds was singing. Soon the crowd gathered, and at once a song was heard. Eagerly the purchasers sought to locate the fine singer. There was something about the song, however, that did not sound just right to the ears of an experienced breeder. My friend stepped to the end of the counter and had a good look. There under the counter was the singing bird: a small boy industriously blowing a bird whistle.

Every year many breeders lose their whole flocks with the disease that is spread by these cheap birds. It is all right to say that only the foolish will buy them, but we have all been caught at one time or another. And many times it is not because the breeder has been foolish in buying these cheap birds, but because they have been brought to him to treat from sources that he had no reason to suspect as being dangerous. I know of one case where several hundreds of dollars worth of stock was lost because the owner shook hands with a man who came to ask advice.

Much has been written on what should be done to meet this condition, but the only real remedy is to be found in a thorough understanding of the disease.

Classification

The disease commonly called Septic Fever in this country and the one under discussion in this article is one of the many forms of *Avian Diphtheria*. It is a totally different disease from *Canary Necrosis* which is often called Septic Fever in English bird literature. This latter disease was described by me under the heading *Hemorrhagic Septicemia* in the April, 1931, issue of the *Roller Canary Journal and Bird World*. This disease now under discussion is identical with Roup, Canker, and Bird Pox in poultry, but in many of the outbreaks germs of the *Hemorrhagic Septicemia* group play an important part.

Etiology

The exact nature of the germ causing *Avian Diphtheria* is unknown. It is so small that it cannot be seen under the most powerful microscope and passes with ease through the pores of a clay filter which will hold back all ordinary bacteria. Germs that can do this are known as filter passers or as filterable virus. The one in question is generally called *Pox Virus* because it is the recognized cause of Bird Pox in poultry. All birds are subject to attack by this virus and it has a very high resistance to disinfectant. Boiling water for 30 minutes does not kill the virus in scabs taken from the pox sores. Five per cent carbolic acid, 2% liquor cresolis, 2% potassium permanganate, 2% copper sulphate, and 1:1000 mercuric chloride all fail to kill the virus in 20 minutes exposure; but it is promptly killed by 2% lye solution.

In every outbreak of this disease that I have seen, deaths have not been due to the action of the virus itself, but to other bacteria which are commonly present on the respiratory and alimentary mucous membranes. For some unknown reason these germs do not, as a rule, have the power to invade the body, but they suddenly take on that power as soon as the diphtheria develops. It is my theory that there is some toxin manufactured by the pox organism that has a stimulating action upon the other bacteria present; although it may be that instead of stimulating the organisms it has a paralyzing effect upon the leucocytes (the white blood cells whose function it is to digest invading bacteria). I have found four different organisms in the blood of birds suffering with this disease. They are

SEPTIC FEVER

Pasteurella avian, the germ of fowl cholera; *Streptococcus pyogenus,* the germ of human erysipelas; *B. Paratyphosus B.,* the germ of paratyphoid; a *pneumococcus* that cannot be distiguished from the germ of human pneumonia by cultural characteristics. The form and course of the disease is always influenced by the nature of this secondary invader, as such germs are called; and I think that death is always due to the secondary invasion. Certain strains of all of these germs mentioned are credited with being the causes of fatal diseases in which the pox virus is not present. One odd feature is that diseases wherein they act as primary causes are much more rapidly fatal than is the diphtheria infection.

Symptoms and Course of the Disease

The first symptoms of *Avian Diphtheria* vary widely in different outbreaks, and in different birds in the same outbreak, making it the easiest of all diseases to recognize when it runs a regular course and the hardest to recognize in irregular cases. The first sign of disease is often that the bird is observed to be breathing too fast, although apparently quite well in all other respects. Several days later his voice may start to change. It drops to a lower and a lower register until it is finally entirely lost. While he continues to sing, or to go through the motions of singing he makes no sound. This condition may exist for a week or more, the only other sign of sickness being that the bird stops to pant once in a while. The panting becomes more frequent and more rapid until the bird is found down at the bottom of the cage gasping for breath. About the time the bird starts to pant the droppings turn yellow. They look just like yellow ochre as it is squeezed from a tube of paint. As the bird gets weak he usually develops diarrhoea, which may be green or bloody just before death. He eats as much as he can, in fact is always hungry in this disease; but in this form cannot swallow much food toward the very last. A bird may live from five days to over one month after showing the first signs of this form of the disease; and that first stage does not develop in less than eight days after exposure, perhaps not until the twenty-first day after exposure. In the form just described an examination of the blood will show the presence of the pneumococcus mentioned above. At the time of death the lungs will have spots of pneumonic consolidation in the stage of gray hepatization. These spots appear to start to develop at the center of the lung at the point where the bronchial tubes enter the wall of the lung, and one or both lungs may be involved. The consolidation is gray, thicker than the unaffected parts of the lung, and extends right through the lung from front to back. Death in this form of disease is usually due to heart failure, and extensive changes are always found in this organ. When the body is opened, the heart appears to be as big as a kidney bean, but it is only because the pericardium is distended with a bloody exudate. When this heart sack is pricked with a lance or needle, the exudate escapes; and it is then seen that the heart is really smaller than normal with its walls very thin. They have been burned up by the long siege of high fever, and they are often perforated so that blood escapes into the heart sack. The liver may be enlarged and reveal some necrosis. There may also be some inflammation of the intestines, but these changes are, as a rule, not enough to make the abdomen appear puffed up. On the contrary, in most cases the abdomen is somewhat shrunken.

SEPTIC FEVER

In another form, this disease may begin with the fast breathing, the yellow droppings, a few ruffled feathers on the head or neck, or a lame foot or wing. Investigation of the ruffled feathers, the foot, or the wing, or whatever part it happens to be, will disclose a very painful sore. Sometimes the sores take the form of fever blisters around the eyes or vent. In some cases the disease develops slowly and in no regular order that will hold for all cases; but the order most usually found is fast breathing, yellow droppings, itching head (the bird is constantly rubbing head on perch or wire of his cage), sores or blisters, abnormal appetite. These stages may all be developed and the bird still able to sing and carry on normal functions. The symptoms may be present for a week or more, the development of the disease progressing slowly. Then, in some cases, the sores develop rapidly until the eyes are closed and the poor creature seems nothing but a mass of sores. In other cases they dry up and start to go away; but in all cases in this form of the disease the bird develops a severe and painful diarrhoea toward the last. The last day or two the droppings may be green or bloody, or they may remain yellow and become so gummy that they foul the feathers and paste up the vent. Death seems to be due to poisons developed by the germs present. The heart and lungs are not greatly changed as a rule. The peritoneum often contains a thin bloody fluid and the liver may, in some cases, be smaller than normal and have a soft jelly-like consistency, the edges being transparent. Or it may be as large as a hickory nut, the outer coating gone, and the elements greatly enlarged and ruptured. This sometimes gives it the appearance of a large rotten mulberry, blue-black in color, although this is not common in this form of the disease. In the early stages of this form of the disease the *streptococcus pyogenus* may be found in the blood and is always found in the sores and blisters. In the later stages *B. Pasteurella* is always found in the blood.

There is another form of this disease that differs from the one just described in that instead of the sores, or perhaps together with them, large bumps will develop on the head. These may make the head appear three times its normal size and are often the first symptoms noted. In other respects this form of the disease progresses just like the one described in the last paragraph. The lumps are yellow and contain a yellow, fibrinous substance resembling fat but very tough.

In still another form of this disease the birds show no symptoms but a badly puffed abdomen, lack of appetite and fluffed feathers. They may die in a few hours or live a day or two. In this form, death usually results from a hemorrhage from the liver, and the liver always shows the mulberry necrosis described above. In these cases, a germ belonging to the hog-cholera group and resembling *B. Paratyphosus B.* in cultural characteristics is found in the blood and liver. There may be some changes in the lungs and heart, but they are not extensive nor so constant as those described in the bronchial form of the disease. This form does not appear often. It is most interesting because it does not differ either in the changes found, nor in the organisms present, from psittacosis in parrots. And inasmuch as psittacosis is also known to be due to a filterable virus, and as it is known that the parrot and canary can transmit the disease from one to the other, I am inclined to believe that they are one and the same disease.

I have described the symptoms and morbid changes most often found in this disease with great detail be-

SEPTIC FEVER

cause of the great importance of an early and correct diagnosis. And in this respect a good rule to follow is that when three birds die or become sick within the first month after you have taken new stock into your bird room, and if any of them has shown any combination of the symptoms mentioned above, it is safe to assume that the outbreak is one of septic fever. Only in characteristic cases is one bird sufficient for a diagnosis.

Treatment

Sanitary measures are of the first importance in this disease. It is necessary to remove the well from the sick if possible. Clean the cages thoroughly and often, and each time inspect each bird for sores and other symptoms of the disease. Wash the cages in strong disinfectant or lye and scrub them well inside and out with a stiff brush. Feed and water the well birds first; always disinfect hands after handling sick birds or tending them. Feed all the green food that they will eat, using wild greens and sod if you can get them. They will eat plenty, too. Give direct sunlight if you can. Feed the regular foods and seed that you have been using. Put glauber salts in all drinking water, strong enough to give it a slightly salty taste. If possible wire for Stroud's Specific at once but if that is impossible or if it is impossible to get it promptly, add three drops of saturated solution of potassium chlorate to each ounce of drinking water along with the salts. Treat the sores by opening them and washing them out with a saturated solution of potassium permanganate, or by injecting the solution into them with a hypodermic needle. These methods will keep the birds alive for a considerable time and will save a great number of them, but they will not save them all or bring the disease under control, as will the specific above mentioned, which was discovered while I was working on this ailment. In treating birds that have the bronchial form of the disease the bird should be kept as quiet as possible and should not be caught or frightened even to clean the cage or to treat sores. The condition of the heart in this form of the disease is such that the least fright may cause death (I have had many of them die in my hand) of a bird that could otherwise be saved. My plan is to treat this form of the disease only with the specific, neglecting the sores, and even the tray and perches where necessary, until the fever is brought under control. Then most of the sores will heal of themselves, and those that do not can be treated with the permanganate.

For several weeks after an outbreak of this disease has been brought under control every bird that has been sick should be inspected for tiny, chronically discharging, water blisters on the head, usually over the beak, although they may be found anywhere on the skull. These small chronic sores carry the virus of the disease for about one month after the fever is broken. Without treatment they will run for years. After one month they do not carry the virus of diphtheria but instead of this the *streptococcus pyogenus*. It is possible for this germ to be transmitted to other birds in the flock and to cause similar sores, and in some cases death. This same germ is often responsible for a sporadic pneumonia in canaries (which comes occasionally but is not generally contagious); so that it is the safest plan to look for the sores and to treat them with the potassium permanganate injection. A single injection large enough to turn the infected area black will cure the sores. A fine sharp pointed needle should be used. It should be inserted into the sore at an angle

SEPTIC FEVER

of about 30 degrees with the surface, and the solution forced in slowly. Take care that the needle does not slip and puncture the skull.

Some Other Methods of Treatment

1. Mix equal parts of sodium citrocarbonate (see list of drugs) and dehydrated sodium phosphate. Add one teaspoonful of this to each quart of drinking water, and after filling the drinker add from ten to twenty drops of commercial peroxide of hydrogen to each ounce drinker. This method of treatment is very satisfactory.

2. Add six grains of copper sulphate to each quart of drinking water given in the mornings. At two P. M. empty the drinkers and refill them with orange juice and let that remain until the birds are put to bed for the night, when the drinkers can again be filled with the sulphate solution. This method is highly recommended, but I have not made use of it myself.

Psittacosis

As I said above, it is my conviction that this disease is due to the action of pox virus. In some of its forms it does not differ in any distinguishable manner from other forms of this disease in other birds. And while it is very hard to treat, it can be cured by an application of the same principles that I have used in curing the disease in other birds. It not infrequently happens that a disease in one animal may be relatively much more dangerous than it is in another species. Thus glanders in horses is very much more dangerous than distemper in dogs, which is the same, or at least a very closely allied disease.

The symptoms of psittacosis in a parrot follow the same course as in a canary. There is fever, fast breathing and the accompanying thirst. The droppings are at first yellow, then become green and bloody, and a very painful diarrhoea precedes death. During the latter stages of the disease the bird will sleep almost all the time except when the diarrhoea forces it to attempt to void droppings, and at such times it may cry out with the pain. In these latter stages the bird refuses both food and drink. It is this fact that makes the disease so hard to treat when the bird happens to be very sick before treatment is attempted.

The following treatment has given 100% cures. Mix Avian Antiseptic and Effervescent Salts in equal parts. Cook up a mush of yellow corn meal or of cracked unhulled rice. Use water enough so that the mush will just be stiff when cold. To one ounce of this add one-fourth teaspoonful of the best honey and a good sized pinch of the treatment. Give this to the bird and coax him to eat it. Do not give him anything to drink. As soon as the bird can be made to eat the food, he will begin to get better; and after three or four days the fever will break and he will be well. He should still be continued on the mush or rice diet, however, but with the medicine left out. Gradually he can be put on a seed diet and given fruit, green food and water.

Where the bird cannot be coaxed to eat at all, it can still sometimes be saved by mixing about two grains of the mixed treatment with one teaspoonful of honey and three of water and feeding it to him a drop at a time with a medicine dropper. Do not force the medicine into the bird; hold the dropper against the side of his bill and let the drops run into his mouth slowly. Only a very sick bird will refuse to taste the honey and to swallow at least a few drops. After one or two doses like this the bird can often be induced to eat the mush. In all other respects the disease in parrots and parrakeets should be treated precisely as described for canaries.

CHAPTER IX

APOPLECTIFORM SEPTICEMIA IN CANARIES
The Results of Some Recent Investigations into the Causes of Fits in Young Canaries

General Discussion

Apoplectiform Septicemia probably causes greater losses among birds of all kinds than any other known disease. It surely causes greater losses among canaries than all other diseases combined and is at the same time the least understood. The name "Apoplectiform" means "like apoplexy" and is applied to the disease under discussion for the reason that in one form the principal symptom of this disease is the paralysis of the wings or feet of the infected bird.

To illustrate how widespread and serious are the losses from this infection it is only necessary to refer to the bird journals. The June, 1930 issue of the *Roller Canary Journal* makes mention of this infection in three places. Mr. Jackson, writing from England, (page 3, continued on page 16) describes "Going Light;" Mrs. Blaylock, page 4, describes "Gastro-Enteritis;" and "Questions and Answers," Q. 1, page 15, gives a case of fits—and even these do not exhaust the description of this infection.

This disease was first described as a disease of poultry by Norgaard and Mohler, Bureau of Animal Industry, 1902, and given the name Apoplectiform septicemia because of its apoplexy-like symptoms. I have been able to find on record no study of the disease in canaries.

Apoplectiform septicemia is due to infection by a specific germ of the type that grows in long chains, which are classified under the generic heading "Streptococci." There are a great many species of streptococci, and they are widely distributed in nature. Some grow in stagnant water, others in decaying food or other decaying organic matter, still others upon the skin and mucous membrane of man and animals. They are commonly associated with infected wounds and lesions in the mouth, throat, lungs, and digestive tract; while some species make their home in the normal intestines.

The species causing Apoplectiform septicemia can be obtained easily in pure cultures from the heart blood of birds that have recently died from the disease, or from blood drawn aseptically from a clipped toe nail of a sick bird during life. It has been by the use of these two methods that I have been able to identify several sets of symptoms as all being forms of one and the same disease.

This organism ordinarily possesses a very low order of virulence for canaries. Birds that have passed the first adult moult are almost entirely immune to this infection and older birds are entirely so. It is only rarely that birds past the first moult are infected, and nestlings under the care of their parents are never attacked, not even when one or both parents have died of the disease. Under like conditions of infection and general management females are more susceptible than males. Most birds are attacked between the time they are weaned and the completion of the baby moult. It is at the very beginning of the baby moult that they are most susceptible, but even at this age a great many are immune. These facts, as well as certain peculiarities associated with the onset of the symptoms of the

APOPLECTIFORM SEPTICEMIA

disease, have been responsible for the great confusion which exists concerning its true nature.

Symptoms and Lesions of the Gastro-Enteritic Form of Apoplectiform Septicemia

In this form of the disease the birds show soft droppings of greenish color, enlarged abdomen with intestines and liver showing through the abdominal wall. Temperature is sub-normal and may be as low as 101 or 102 degrees F., the normal temperature of a canary in perfect health and breeding condition being 107½ degrees F. The bird fluffs its feathers, shivers often and looks generally very miserable, although it continues to eat. The onset of the attack is almost always coincident with a sudden change in the weather. If the bird lives several days, the following lesions will be found upon post mortem examination: Inflammation of the intestines, particularly the upper portion; enlargement of the liver (there may be yellow necrotic spots in this organ if death has been somewhat delayed). Hemorrhages may be found in the abdominal cavity. But the most characteristic lesion is an enlarged spleen, the surface of which is very dark and covered with a peculiar mottling. Where death has been long delayed, this organ may be one-eighth of an inch in diameter and from three-fourths to one inch long. Upon section it will show a soft gray pulp with a black core extending lengthwise through its center.

Acute Hemorrhagic Form

In this form of Apoplectiform septicemia a bird will seem perfectly well and in splendid condition, although perhaps highly nervous. Suddenly and without warning the bird is seized by a violent fit. It flies wildly about the cage or room for a few moments, then falls to the floor and lies either limp or twitching. The bird may die in the first fit; it may even be dead when it hits the floor. In such cases post mortem will reveal a major hemorrhage, usually discharging into the pericardium (heart sac) or peritoneum (abdominal sac), though this hemorrhage may discharge into an air sac in one of the bones or into the brain or spinal cord.

The bird may not die during the first fit, but instead may get up, look dazed for a few moments, and then seem perfectly well again, only to have the attack repeated within a day or two. Any one of these attacks may prove fatal, but birds have suffered from them in rare cases for as long as one year and then entirely recovered and made good singers and breeders. In some cases the birds come out of the fit paralyzed in one leg or wing. This is due to a hemorrhage in the brain, cord, or tissue which causes pressure upon the motor nerve leading to the affected part. The paralysis will cure itself in time if the disease does not prove fatal.

The morbid anatomy in the hemorrhagic form of the disease differs little from that found in the gastro-enteritic form where death is delayed, but where death is sudden there are likely to be few departures from normal. The liver and spleen will be but slightly enlarged though the latter will always display the characteristic mottling of the surface noted in other forms of the disease. This mottling is due to the enlargement of the normally invisible blood vessels of the organ and their engorgement with very dark blood.

It is notable in the chronic hemorrhagic or epileptic form of this disease that the first attack is usually set off by a loud noise or some sudden fright and that future attacks are usually set off by the same external stimulus.

Immunity

It has been reported (Norgaard and Mohler, Bureau of Animal Industry, 1902) that fowls may be immunized against this disease by the intravenous injection of killed cultures of the organism involved. I have not tested this on canaries due to the fact that there is such a high natural immunity in this bird that it would be difficult to judge the effect of the injection, which in itself would be very difficult to make upon such a small bird.

Prevention consists of good management and perfect sanitation. The avoidance of all predisposing causes, which include anything that will lower the birds' vitality; and paying strict attention to the probable sources of infection, decaying soft foods and stale water. All egg products should be thoroughly sterilized before using. Recently this disease broke out in a flock kept under perfectly sanitary conditions. I was able to isolate the organism of the disease from a sample of cod liver oil emulsion in which raw egg yolk had been used as the emulsifying agent.

Treatment

The usual advice to feed birds bread and milk and to give maw seed is good. It will cure birds only slightly infected, but under circumstances of very heavy infection there will be many birds whom this treatment will not help. All physics and laxative tonics must be strictly avoided. Avian Antiseptic given in the drinking water every other day will stop the spread of the disease and will cure some cases. Peroxide of hydrogen given in the drinking water, one part of the commercial three percent solution of peroxide of hydrogen to nine parts of water, given every other day is also good but more expensive. Waterbury's tonic, one ounce; tincture of opium, one dram; tincture of gentian, one dram; Aromatic Cascara, one dram; and pure grain alcohol to make up to three ounces is a very valuable prescription in the treatment of this disease. The dose is from three to ten drops in the ounce of drinking water. When this tonic is used every other day and Avian Antiseptic on the alternate days, all birds, even though very heavily infected, may be saved. For these good results, however, some judgment is necessary. Treatment of badly infected birds must be continued for some time and discontinued gradually at larger and larger intervals, first one day, then two, then three, etc., if a relapse is to be avoided. The above prescription can be filled by any good prescription druggist, but he can only fill it upon presentation of a prescription, signed by a doctor or veterinarian licensed to prescribe narcotic drugs.

CHAPTER X

INFECTIOUS NECROSIS OF CANARIES

This is a form of hemorrhagic septicemia that is confined to canaries and other small seed eating birds. It is not common in this country except where it has been introduced by imported birds.

Etiology

The cause of infectious necrosis is a germ belonging to the hemorrhagic septicemia group. It differs from the germ of fowl cholera in that it is slightly larger and will not cause disease in chickens, pigeons, sparrows, and finches, though mice, rabbits, and guinea pigs are susceptible. The differentiation of this disease from Fowl Cholera is much simpler by means of the symptoms and lesions (changes brought about in the body by the development of the disease) produced than by studying the germ. The incubation period of the disease is from three to five days.

Symptoms

There is nothing in the symptoms of this disease that is typical unless the very fact that there are no well defined symptoms like those found in most of the other septicemic diseases is itself characteristic. The bird refuses food, gets very weak, and finally sits on the bottom of the cage and dies. The sick bird lives from 24 to 36 hours after the onset of the disease. There is fever, but I do not know of any one ever measuring it. I myself have not done so.

Morbid Anatomy

It is when the abdomen is opened that the real nature of this disease is revealed. The spleen is greatly swollen and knotty or warty looking. There are a great many nodules of a yellow color, and the organ is so fragile that it will break up when being removed. The liver contains a great many of these yellow nodules which vary in size from mere points to the size of a pin head, rape seed, or even larger. There may be yellow nodules in the throat which are easily detached from the surrounding tissue. Those in the liver are not easily detached. This disease might be mistaken for tuberculosis if the morbid anatomy alone were considered, but tuberculosis is a chronic disease. Birds in which well developed nodules are found will have been in poor condition for some time and only the older birds will be affected.

Treatment

Potassium permanganate in the drinking water strong enough to turn it a wine red and about two grains of sodium sulphate added to each ounce drinker has been recommended. One writer reports the cure of contagious bird diseases (his description is, however, more like that of septic fever than of infectious necrosis, though these are often confused even in name) by the use of one teaspoonful of brandy, a few drops of paregoric, and a little red pepper in the drinking water. He was not writing for the American breeder. The more authoritative writers recommend "kill and disinfect" as the only known measure of control. I have met with this disease only a few times, but in every case treatment with Avian Antiseptic in the drinking water proved effective. When treated as septic fever (avian diphtheria) with both the antiseptic and effervescent mixture, all sick birds die and no influence is noted on the spread of the disease; while the same is true of septic fever if the antiseptic is given in the drinking water. This difference is believed to be due to the fact that the reaction of the antiseptic is influenced by the chemical reaction of the blood. It was first thought to be due to the fact that in some diseases the bird did not eat, but this has been found not to be the case; for in the one class the disease is cured when the antiseptic alone is put into the beak, while in the other both the antiseptic and the salts mixture must be given to get satisfactory results.

CHAPTER XI

HEMORRHAGIC SEPTICEMIA IN CANARIES

General Discussion

Hemorrhagic Septicemia is the name given to a large class of contagious diseases afflicting a wide range of animals and birds. Cattle, hogs, rabbits, sheep, and all the domesticated birds are subject to attacks by one or more diseases belonging to this group. The symptoms and lesions vary somewhat with the species infected, but changes in the blood and hemorrhages into the tissues of one or more organs are a general characteristic of this group of diseases. Point-like hemorrhages discharging into the heart, upper intestines, liver, or fatty tissues are almost always present and a jelly-like exudate discharging into the pericardium, peritoneum, under the skin in cattle—into the air sac in birds—is another common feature of hemorrhagic septicemias. This jelly-like exudate gives the impression that the blood has turned to jelly. These two features of these diseases are responsible for the name "Hemorrhagic Septicemia"—meaning an infection characterized by hemorrhages.

Etiology

In all cases of hemorrhagic septicemia an examination of the blood reveals a small oval, rod-like organism that does not stain evenly with aniline dyes. The organisms are somewhat "O-shaped," and when stained look as the "O" would look if shaded at the ends instead of on the sides as we usually shade the letter "O". The members of this group of germs vary only

HEMORRHAGIC SEPTICEMIA

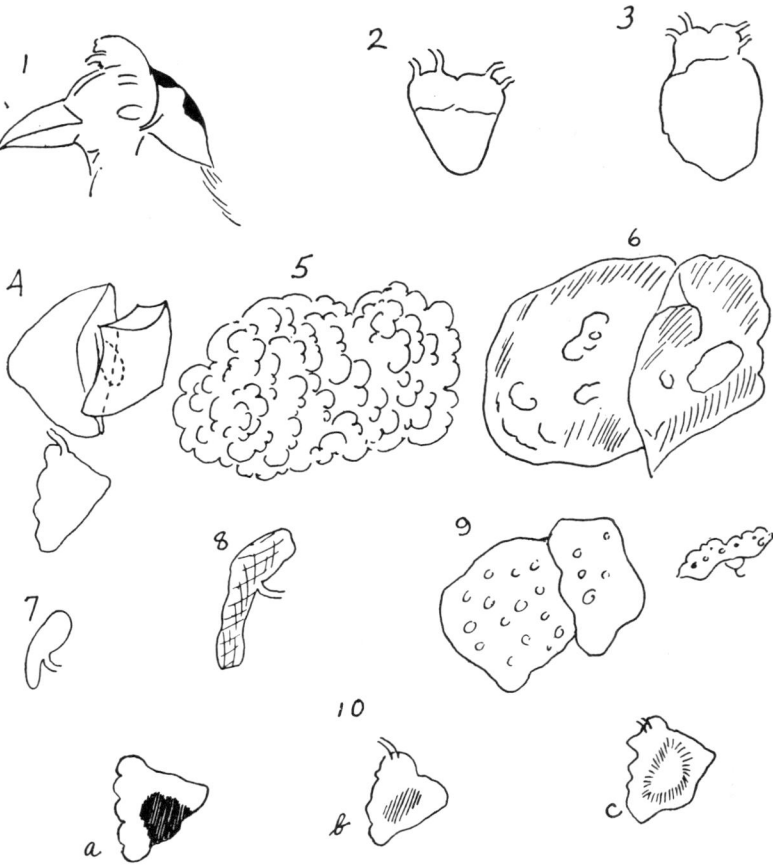

1. Head of a bird that died of fit. Bright red hemorrhagic spots on skull indicate apoplectiform septicemia.

2. Normal heart 1½ times normal size.

3. Heart sac from bird that died of septic fever, showing greatly increased size due to pericarditis. The heart itself is not enlarged.

4. Normal liver about 1½ times normal size. Gall is attached to right lobe and under left lobe. Lung normal size.

5. Mulberry liver from psittacosis, only slightly enlarged.

6. Liver showing gray, leathery necrotic spots from apoplectiform septicemia.

7. Spleen, normal.

8. Spleen from bird dead with apoplectiform septicemia.

9. Liver and spleen, showing lumpy surface due to tubercular nodules.

10. Pneumonic lesions
    a—dark purple, normal thickness.
    b—thin red spot.
    c—blue gray, greatly thickened.

slightly in the nature of their growth on media or in their biochemical properties. For these reasons there is some doubt as to whether all these diseases are due to one germ which varies widely in virulence (the power to cause disease) or to a group of organisms composed of a great number of distinct species that differ only in their power to cause disease and, slightly, in their size, shape, and cultural characteristics. The first view is supported by the fact that there are great variations in virulence within a single strain infecting a single species of animal; the second by the fact that it is only rarely that members of one species of animal will take the disease from another species.

This germ or group of germs, as the case may be, has been given the name *Pasteurella*. The most common member of the group attacking birds, the fowl cholera organism, is called *Bacterium Pasteurella Avian*.

There are at least two and perhaps three forms of hemorrhagic septicemia known in canaries. The first and most important in this country is fowl cholera; the second, a common disease in Germany, is called "Infectious Necrosis."

Fowl Cholera in Canaries

This disease is more common in canaries than is generally suspected, though it is rarely found in well treated flocks. It is most common in birds that have been shipped about a great deal and kept under unsanitary conditions. The disease takes on three forms: peracute, acute, and chronic.

Symptoms

In the peracute form the bird puffs up suddenly, gets very weak, shows a high fever, and sleeps a great deal but continues to eat and drink. On inspection the

HEMORRHAGIC SEPTICEMIA

abdomen may be found to be a deep purple in color and greatly swollen, or it may be reddened. The disease continues only a few hours before the bird falls dead either from the perch or while it is hopping about the cage. In other peracute cases the abdomen will be reddened and have a corrugated appearance; this is also true in most acute and chronic cases.

The most noticeable symptom in acute, as well as in chronic cases, is the yellow color of the droppings which are a dull yellow, of pasty consistency, and resemble more than anything else a cheap grade of yellow ochre as put up in tubes for school art work. The matter consists of urates and mucous; and while this is the most constant of all symptoms, in both cholera and diphtheria, there is considerable variation in the color and consistency of the discharge. It may be green, brown, or a clear, viscous fluid. In some cases, though not in many, the droppings are bloody.

The bird eats almost until the time of death, but chooses soft food rather than seed. It will also be found picking the sand in the bottom of the cage as if looking for something that will give it relief, and will eat burnt matches, paper, and other unusual things. The temperature in the early stages of the disease may be as high as 113 degrees F., but in the latter stages before death it may fall as low as 96 degrees F. The bird is fluffed up and spends much time sleeping in the bottom of the cage.

Morbid Anatomy

In the peracute form there will be as a rule very few changes found at post mortem examination. There are almost always punctiform hemorrhages found in the heart and the first two sections of the upper intestines. But in some few cases there will be extensive changes. There may be a mulberry liver. The outer covering of the organ is entirely destroyed and the necrotic changes make the organ look like a big rotten mulberry. In such cases there will be a serous exudate, often mixed with blood, in the peritoneum. There may be a bloody, fibrinous exudate or a gelatinous exudate in the pericardium. The lungs may show hemorrhagic pneumonia in chronic cases, but changes in the lungs are not common in this disease in canaries.

Immunity

There are methods of immunization that are recommended for live stock: cattle, sheep, hogs, and rabbits; but these have not given much success in birds and are impractical and unnecessary in canaries. They consist of injections of killed cultures of a strain of the same germ that has lost its power to produce the disease (this through heating or through prolonged artificial cultivation), or by the use of products made from the exudates of the disease.

Treatment

The treatment of Fowl Cholera is exactly the same as that of septic fever, excepting that the disease is neither as contagious, as insidious, or as hard to treat as diphtheria. In many outbreaks of this disease the only treatment needed is to give the birds a good tonic and plenty of black loam earth. They will eat the earth and seem to find something in it that kills the germs in the bowels. Sulphate of iron (copperas) in the drinking water is said to be effective. The dose recommended is six grains to each quart of water used. I.Q.S. (iron, quinine, and strychnine) tonic as put up for human use, given three drops to the ounce of drinking water, is of some value in treating this disease in ca-

HEMORRHAGIC SEPTICEMIA

naries where the outbreak is not of an especially virulent nature. Stroud's Specific stamps out the disease within 48 hours. But regardless of the treatment that is used, it should never be forgotten that the first factor in avoiding losses from any contagious disease consists of improved sanitation. Washing the equipment in water that is so hot the hands can just be put into it is enough to kill the germs of this disease, as they have very little resistance to either heat or disinfectants.

CHAPTER XII

NESTLING DIARRHOEA

A Discussion of Some of the Causes Responsible for a High Rate of Mortality Among Young Canaries[1]

General Discussion

From California we have a letter which says: "I have been raising birds for 36 years. My birds are all looking fine but like nearly all roller birds this year the old birds are starving the young. I have had to raise the babies by hand feeding."

A lady in Iowa writes: "I hope that you can tell me what is wrong with my birds. The young die on the fifth day. The old birds feed them as long as they will eat, but still there seems to be something wrong with the old birds for only the young of certain pairs seem to be affected. Many old breeders in this locality have not been able to raise a single bird so far this year."

A lady in Mississippi writes: "I do not know what is wrong with my birds this year. I never had any trouble before, but this year the old birds have let almost all of the young die. I have raised some by hand."

---

[1]Investigation of the cases mentioned at the heading of this article (which continued for a considerable time after the article was written) as well as of a large number of other cases, has definitely shown that the trouble was in every case due to the food; and in almost every case the cause was either stale hemp seed or stale canary seed. When these breeders had been supplied with good seed, the trouble vanished as if by magic. The same birds that had lost every chick before raised full nests for the rest of the season.

NESTLING DIARRHOEA

A man in Chicago writes: "I am losing all of my hens with what I think is septic fever. During the first nest the hen gets a stringy, foul smelling diarrhoea. The droppings soon turn watery; the bird gets very weak and dies. I have written to all of the authorities but have been able to get no advice that would help me control the trouble."

The condition commonly known as nestling diarrhoea, sweating hens, and poor feeding mothers has never been very closely studied so far as I can find from an exhaustive research of bird literature. I do not mean that nothing has been written upon the subject, but that what has been written is largely in the form of opinions which may or may not have any basis in fact so far as the causes are concerned. Some breeders ascribe everything to poor management; others blame "hereditary weakness" for all of the trouble; still others put all the blame on certain foods. Green food is one of the articles of diet that comes in for most adverse criticism.

Symptoms

In the most common form of nestling diarrhoea, it is first noticed that the hen sits very closely on the nest and that her breast feathers are matted as if she had been sweating. The nest will be found damp and foul and the fuzz on the young birds matted down. The young will be weak and bloodless. The hen's droppings are of a light dirty cream color, of stringy consistency and have a foul odor. Her abdomen is found to be somewhat enlarged and the intestines can be seen through the wall. The young die from the third to the tenth day. Some few may live. As a rule the hen does not die. There is nothing distinctive, outside of the evidence of starvation or indigestion, found in the body of the chick. Post mortem examination of the hen will show an extensive catarrhal inflammation of the intestines. The body is likely to be in a weakened condition but most of the organs are normal. Blood cultures are mostly sterile, and where bacteria are found in the blood they are of a low order of virulence.

Causes

Symptoms as described above may be due to the feeding of poor seed; mustard seed instead of rape, musty canary seed or rancid hemp seed; they may be due to the hen's taking putrid matter into her system while cleaning the nest; they may be due to damp, filthy cages, stale green food, or stale soft food; they may be due to excessive mite infestation. The causes are not constitutional at the time the trouble first makes its appearance, although they may become so if neglected.

Treatment

Remove the cause. Feed only good tested seed. Get rid of the mites. Keep the trays and dishes clean. Correct the diet to be sure that the birds are getting the vitamines necessary for growth and reproduction. Give all the green food that they can eat. Wild greens are best. They should be given twice each day. Sod-grass, given roots, earth, and all, is very good at this time. If it is always given to all birds feeding chicks there will be little trouble from bowel infections. The old birds will eat the black loam from around the roots of the grass and seem to find something in it that will cause digestive and bowel disorders to clear up. Only grass from clean ground should be used—never that from a poultry yard. Many recommend bread and milk for this trouble, but I think that every breeder who leaves milk out of his bird's diet will be better off. Hens will feed it, to be sure, but its use is very apt to lower the health and production record of any flock. Stroud's Specific will act as a stop-gap in such ailments, but medical treatment is not, as a rule, indicated.

Thrush

Thrush is an infection of the mouth, nose, and crop due to an organism closely related to the moulds to which has been given the name of *Oidium Albicans*. This same organism causes disease of the mouth in poultry, turkeys, pigeons, and children. Other animals may be attacked, but I have not been able to find any account of this happening. I have not been able to find a report of a study of this infection in canaries, but have found the disease in a considerable number of cases. The lesions of the disease consist of yellow, gray or whitish patches growing on the mucous membrane of the mouth and crop. Birds infected with thrush fungus cannot feed their young. They often have asthmatic symptoms. This disease is mentioned here not because it is in any way related to nestling diarrhoea, but because it is likely to be the cause of losses that are ascribed to nestling diarrhoea. The condition can be treated with Avian Antiseptic in the drinking water, with iodide of potassium in the drinking water (three drops of saturated solution to the ounce of water), or by irrigating the crop with a solution of boric acid. This is recommended for large birds. It is not so easy to treat a canary in this way.

Bacillery White Diarrhoea

Bacillery White Diarrhoea is a fatal septicemia of baby chicks, principally incubated chicks. Other birds are not known to be susceptible to it; but there have been so many of the symptoms and lesions of this disease described to me in reports of the loss of nestling canaries this season that I have come to suspect that possibly canaries are susceptible to it, and add the following in the hope that it will stimulate investigation and perhaps furnish a basis for observations.

Etiology

Bacillery White Diarrhoea is a fatal septicemia of baby chicks due to infection with a slender rod-like organism that has been given the name *Bacterium Pullorum*. In rare cases this germ attains a virulence that will permit it to cause a fatal septicemia in adult fowls, but as a rule old birds are not susceptible to an acute attack of disease due to this organism.

Symptoms and General Characteristics

While old birds as a rule do not have the disease in the acute form, those that have had the disease as chicks, and have recovered, carry the germ throughout life. The disease is localized in the ovaries of the female and the germ is passed on to the chick in the egg. After the eggs hatch and during the period when the yolk is being absorbed into the system, the general infection takes place. The first signs of sickness are usually noted at the end of the third day of life. The disease is very contagious among chicks at this age and those that do not have the germ in their systems are quickly infected by those that have. Losses run to about 70 percent in infected broods, but of those chicks that have survived the first week without infection a considerable number will not die of the disease. These grow up to provide carriers for the germ and to pass it on to the next generation. Not all chicks hatched from the eggs of hens infected with this organism carry the disease. The chicks droop the wings, eat less than normal, ruffle the feathers, and look generally miserable. They soon develop a soft, whitish, pasty diarrhoea. The matter voided often adheres to the feathers around the vent, blocking the opening. The abdomen is greatly enlarged and as a rule very dark in color. In acute cases the chick soon falls to the floor and dies, but in other cases it may remain standing for some time. Often in these more chronic cases the feet swell. Sometimes the swelling is confined to one foot; sometimes both are affected. Deaths continue from the end of the first week until well into the third or fourth week after hatching.

Morbid Anatomy

Since Bacillery White Diarrhoea is a purely septicemic disease there are no well defined and constant changes found at autopsies performed on baby chicks dead from it. The most constant divergence from the normal condition is the fact that the egg yolk as a rule has not been entirely absorbed. The liver is often greatly enlarged and of a yellow color; or it may be dark in color with bands or lacings of a golden yellow around the edges of the organ. These conditions, the history of the disease, and the absence of the lesions of aspergillosis or coccidiosis, are usually enough to establish the diagnosis. The organism of the disease is easily obtained in pure culture from the blood or organs of birds dead of it.

The presence of chronic Bacillery Pullorum infection in a breeding hen is detected during life by a blood test or a bacterin reaction that has been developed for that purpose. Examination of the ovary of an infected hen will reveal a large number of misshapen ova (yolks in formation). Some are angular, while others may be pear shaped. Normal ova are round. Any irregularity is evidence of disease.

Treatment

There is no generally recognized treatment for Bacillery White Diarrhoea. The disease in baby chicks is easily controlled by the use of Avian Antiseptic in the drinking water. There is some reason for believing that the chronic infection in breeding hens may be curable, but more study is necessary before we can be sure of this.

CHAPTER XIII

AN UNIDENTIFIED DISEASE OF CANARIES

In August, 1929, issue of *The Roller Canary Journal and Bird World* I described a contagious disease of canaries that I then thought to be identical with typhoid in fowls. The limited number of studies that I have been able to make of the disease since that time have left grave doubts in my mind as to the correctness of that conclusion.

Characterization. The disease is an acute, contagious septicemia attacking canaries and sparrows. It is not a very common disease and for that reason I have been unable to give it the study required for complete identification. I have reports of several out-breaks of the disease following the purchase of new stock and an equal number of reports of the disease where no new stock had been brought into the bird room; the only cases that I myself have studied were the result of sporadic outbreaks.

Etiology. The cause of this disease is a bacterium which closely resembles *B. Sanguinarium* and *B. Pullorum* (See section on Bacteriology) in its growth on gelatin and agar stab cultures. I was not able to continue my cultivations far enough to identify it positively with or definitely to differentiate it from either of the germs named. This is regrettable, for an identification of the germ causing the disease might give some suggestions as to its mode of propagation and also indicate methods by which the infection could be controlled.

Symptoms. While I have been unable to identify this disease from its germ, the disease itself is very easily recognizable from the symptoms. The first day the bird fluffs up its feathers, breathes a little faster than usual, sits all bunched up and sleeps most of the time. This first day the bird may stand on only one foot. It eats little but drinks a great deal. The bowels are loose and the discharge is watery.

The second day the bird eats nothing at all and drinks very little. It hardly ever leaves the perch and now sleeps on two feet and is very weak. The droppings become thick, white, and chalky. The disease progresses very rapidly and the bird either soon falls from the perch and dies, or having left the perch is unable to get back and sits on the bottom of the cage and dies. Death comes within from 12 to 48 hours after the first symptom is noted, and what information I have indicates that there is not more than 48 hours between the time of exposure and the development of the symptoms.

Morbid Anatomy. The most characteristic change noted in this disease is in the liver, which may be increased to five times its normal size. When the body is picked the only abnormal symptom noted is a greatly enlarged abdomen. When this is opened, the liver forces its way out, showing it has been retained under considerable pressure. It is very probable that this pressure on the heart is responsible for the rapid progress of the disease to its fatal termination. The outer coating of the liver is intact and the organ has a smooth shining surface. The general color is dark reddish-brown, somewhat darker than normal. There may be small point-like hemorrhages within the liver itself, but there is none discharging into the peritoneum. One very noticeable characteristic of this disease is the appearance of golden yellow bands or lacings along the edges of the liver. As a rule these are not exactly on the edges but at a distance of one millimeter or more from the edges and parallel to them.

The intestines are inflamed in the upper portion and at times there are punctiform hemorrhages visible to the naked eye.

The kidneys are likely to be slightly enlarged and a little lighter in color than usual in normal specimens.

The spleen may be enlarged and have necrotic spots, but this is not a constant symptom. The heart and lungs appear normal to the naked eye.

The blood is clotted and lighter than is normal. There are no hemorrhages or exudates into any of the serous cavities.

Treatment. As said above, this disease is highly contagious. The same control measures that were recommended for septic fever should be put into effect at once. The difficulty of control in this disease is due to the fact that it is so rapid in its spread that half of the aviary may be wiped out before one gets control measures into operation. On the other hand the short period of incubation and the short duration of the disease operate to the breeders' advantage; for once the disease is stopped, it is stopped for good as a rule. Medical treatment of the sick offers little hope of success because death ensues almost before the treatment has a chance to act. Stroud's Specific will cure the disease, but in order to insure this result, the antiseptic or the antiseptic and salts mixed in equal proportions must be given in drinking water as strong as the birds will drink it. It must be given to the whole flock and will stamp out the disease in forty-eight hours, usually stopping all losses from the very first dose. I do not know of any other treatment that has ever been used successfully for this disease. There are reasons for thinking that potassium chlorate, three drops of saturated solution to each ounce of drinking water; peroxide of hydrogen, ten drops of the commercial solution to each ounce of drinking water, or calcium permanganate, three drops of the saturated solution to the ounce of drinking water, might be effective. All of these substances are powerful oxidizing antiseptics.

CHAPTER XIV

ASPERGILLOSIS IN CANARIES

A Highly Fatal Disease Due to the Use of Moldy Food

General Discussion

Aspergillosis is the name given to a disease that is caused by infection with a pathogenic fungus (mould) which commonly grows on grain, seeds, and other vegetable matter that has been exposed to damp, and which belongs to the class of mould growths that are classified under the name *Aspergillus*.

There are about 200 species of aspergillus fungi. They are the common food moulds, but only about three species are pathogenic (able to cause disease in man or animals), and only one species, *Aspergillus Fumigatus,* is known to cause serious losses. This species causes disease and death in man, animals, and all species of domesticated birds.

The spores of aspergillus fumigatus are very often found in the dust from rye and canary seed, and the disease is brought about by these spores being inhaled into the respiratory system and growing upon the respiratory mucous membrane.

Aspergillus Pneumo-mycosis (brooder pneumonia) is a common acute disease of baby chicks, some species of parrots, and has been found in both cattle and man; but usually the disease in birds is confined to the air sacs and air tubes and is chronic in course, the lungs remaining uninfected up to the very last.

It may be well to explain here, for the benefit of those unfamiliar with the anatomy of birds, that in addition to the lungs and bronchi, (which make up the

ASPERGILLUS FUMIGATUS

respiratory system in animals) birds have an extensive system of air tubes and air sacs that extend throughout the body and into several of the important bones. All of these tubes and cavities are connected with the bronchial tubes and lungs and are used in breathing. This fact probably has much to do with the long, powerful notes that our rollers are able to bring, and it certainly provides an ideal opportunity for germs and spores to find lodgment in the respiratory tract. This is especially true where the bird is deprived of its normal amount of flying exercise.

ASPERGILLOSIS

Morbid Anatomy

The mould may develop in any place where the spores of this fungus find lodgment in the respiratory system. The growth may be confined to a single air cell or be spread over a large portion of the respiratory mucous membrane. This membrane when in healthy condition is very thin and transparent. The mould growing upon it makes it thick and opaque. The growth is grey or green in color and has a musty or mouldy odor. In some cases merely the surface of the sacs and tubes is covered with a thin growth while in others some of the air sacs may be completely filled by it. Growth inside of a bone may destroy all of the bone but the thin, hard, outer coating, and may even cause that to bulge out of shape. In some advanced cases the growth will penetrate the walls of blood vessels; the spores are thus carried to all parts of the body and may set up necrotic lesions almost anywhere. The kidneys are more often infected in this manner than are the other organs.

Symptoms

There are no regular well defined symptoms in this disease. In the acute cases where the lungs are infected there are the usual symptoms of pneumonia; including rapid breathing, fever, great weakness, lack of appetite, great loss of bodily heat, and death. There is usually diarrhoea before death.

In chronic cases the disease is well advanced before there are any symptoms whatever, and then the symptoms vary with the location and extent of the growth. If the lesions are situated in the trachea or bronchi (wind pipe or bronchial tubes) there will be hoarseness and wheezing, and we have a typical case of asthma (which is not a disease but a symptom).

If the lesions are situated inside one of the bones we have what may be called a case of cancer; and when they are situated in the abdominal or thoracic air saes, the only early symptom may be the gradual loss of weight and pep and we have a case of going light. These chronic symptoms do not differ greatly from those of tuberculosis or coccidiosis.

Diagnosis

There is no certain method of diagnosing aspergillosis during the life of the infected bird, excepting that it may be suspected where the conditions are right for its development. A careful examination of the air sacs and the tubes after death will usually be all that is necessary to establish the identity of the infection, but there will be doubtful cases that can only be identified by the microscope or the culture tube. If a small piece of infected tissue or exudate is placed on acid agar and the tube kept at blood heat and in the dark for 24 hours, the surface will be covered with a characteristic fuzzy white growth.

Treatment

There is no recognized treatment known for this disease. All the authorities that I have looked up report that once the disease is established the result is always fatal. It has been claimed by one contemporary that parrots suffering with acute aspergillus pneumomycosis may be cured by the use of the new and powerful antiseptic, Chinosol, in the drinking water. Dosage is not given. (Chinosol is a chemical substance which comes as a yellow powder and is used as a douche in solution of one to five thousand parts of water. A solution for internal use might have to be still weaker than this.)

Internal mycosis (the term 'mycosis' is applied to

ASPERGILLOSIS

any diseased condition due to mould infection regardless of the species of fungus involved) in human subjects is treated by the intravenous injection of potassium or sodium iodide in doses ranging from 10 to 30 grains every 24 hours. Actinomycosis (lumpy jaw) in cattle is always promptly and permanently cured by the internal administration of potassium iodide.

Some Interesting Cases

About two years ago I received 12 birds that were suspected of Aspergillus infection. They were canaries, one year old and of both sexes. All were in good flesh, and some were really too fat, but all were sick. They were puffed up and did not respond to good care or the usual tonics. One female was killed. In the pleura and on the surface of one lung were noticed some slight gray green patches that were hardly noticeable. Scrapings of these spots, made with a flamed needle, were seeded on agar. Cultures were made from the blood and organs. Those from the pleura scrapings developed the characteristic aspergillus growth. All others remained sterile. The remaining birds were treated for two weeks with potassium iodide, 3 drops of saturated solution to the ounce of drinking water. All recovered. Ten months later one of these birds became lame in one wing. It was a hen that I was breeding. She had raised one nest and built the second when one morning she was unable to get up to her nest. She built another in the bottom of the cage, laid her eggs in it and began sitting. She continued to feed chicks from her first nest. It was thought that the bird had broken or hurt her wing while building her second nest. When after a reasonable time the wing did not heal, the eggs were given to another hen and the crippled bird examined. A large growth was found in one wing and the bird killed. The main tumor was in the humerus (the largest bone in the wing), but the ulna and metacarpus (the bones that carry the flight feathers) were also infected. The tumor was about ¼-inch thick by ⅜-inch long. The smaller bones were honey-combed with the mould growth. The bones of the other wing were infected and in very bad condition, but the bird had shown no lameness in that wing. There was no question as to the diagnosis. It was a true case of mould growth. It was checked by cultures, however.

Two months later, right at the end of the breeding season, another hen went out of condition. She was treated with Avian Antiseptic and got better, only to drag on half sick and half well. Sometime later she became lame for a few days and was again treated with the antiseptic. After a week's treatment she could fly fairly well. Finally the bird was killed. Both wings were infected and the bone structures almost destroyed. There were large cheesy growths in each shoulder at the point where the air tube passed from the thorax to the wing bone. These were brownish yellow in color, rather tough and easily separated from the covering tissue. One was as large as a hulled oat grain and pear-shaped; one the size of a BB shot and others the size of large rape seeds.

In thinking the matter over, I recalled that both of these hens had carried their wings in a drooping manner for some time before they showed any other symptoms of illness. It was also noticed that two other birds from the same lot were carrying their wings in a drooping manner. They were carefully examined and it was found that one, a male, was in poor bodily condition, while the other, a female, was in perfect bodily condition. A pronounced thickening of the humerus of one wing was noted in the male, and in his other wing and in both of the hen's wings there seemed to be some thickening of the bone.

These birds were kept under treatment for three months. For one week they were given Avian Antiseptic in their water every day—1 grain to the ounce of water—the second week they were given three drops of saturated solution of potassium iodide to each ounce of drinking water. These treatments were given alternately, one week the antiseptic, the next the potassium iodide, until both birds seemed to be in perfect condition. The wing bones returned to normal, but it has now been six months since treatment was discontinued and both birds are still in first class condition, and are breeding, yet both still droop the wings. There is no way of determining with certainty that these two birds had aspergillosis but the observations are given for what they are worth.

Infection

Aspergillosis is an infective disease since exudates taken from the body of a bird suffering from the disease, introduced into the body of a well bird will set up a diseased condition in the well bird; but it is not contagious in the sense that the serious bacterial diseases are contagious. The sick can be caged for months with the well without danger of the well birds being infected from them. So long as the birds are kept in clean cages, given plenty of light and air, and are fed on fresh, clean, dust-free seeds, there is absolutely no danger from aspergillosis. In fact, infection appears to take place only when the bird is exposed to the very worst conditions; dusty, mouldy seed, and damp, dark cages.

CHAPTER XV

MY BIRD IS DEAD
An Introduction to Diagnosis

"My bird is dead. Why did he die? I treated him well, but he puffed up for a couple of days and then died. Please tell me why?" Every breeder who has ever written anything on the care of birds has had many such questions put to him. And it is not only the novice who is the offender in this respect. Breeders of years of experience often ask advice on the cause of their losses, giving little more information than is indicated above upon which to base a diagnosis. There is some excuse for the young offender, but little excuse for the old breeder, who should be trained in observing the actions of his birds, and should be able to note anything abnormal either in the bird's actions or anatomy. Very few seem to be able to do this and the only thing to which this failure can be ascribed is carelessness in the use of the eyes.

The Observation of Symptoms

Any sort of abnormal conduct on the part of a bird may be the first sign of sickness. If a bird seems to stop in his singing and pant, it may mean that he is too hot and it may mean that he has a fever. If his voice suddenly changes key, it may be the first sign of diphtheria. If a bird that is usually steady and friendly gets highly nervous and jumps in fright when there is nothing unusual to scare him, it is almost certain to mean that something is wrong with him. If a tonic has been given, it will probably mean that he is suffering from strychnine poisoning. In other cases it may mean food poisoning or apoplectiform septicemia. In some diseases a bird eats, but less than normal; in others he eats more than normal; and in still others he does not eat at all. In most diseases the bird puffs out his feathers, but not in all, at least not in the first stages. In diphtheria during the early stages, the feathers may be carried more closely than in health; this may be true in cholera also. The attempt here, however, is not to give a list of symptoms and diseases, but to point out the importance of watching for little things, making mental note of them and remembering them later if they should be followed by the death of the bird; for it is by such mental associations that one learns to differentiate between ailments. Isolated symptoms are often common to many diseases, so that it is only by a certain grouping of various symptoms that the specific disease can be determined.

Next to the actions of the bird the droppings give an important indication as to his health. Normally they are black with white ends. The black portion is the faeces from the digestive tract while the white is urine from the kidneys. Any change in the color of either of these portions is almost sure to mean that there is something wrong unless the color can be directly attributed to certain foods not contained in the regular diet. In this connection it must be remembered that foods, especially their coloring, may be reflected in the color of the faeces but never in the color of the urine. Changes that should be looked for are not merely those of color but also in the amount of droppings and their consistency. In sporadic pneumonia the droppings will be very scant, of a reddish-brown color, and of a thick, dry consistency. In diphtheria and cholera they will be sulphur-colored, of thick, gummy consistency, and foul smelling. In typhoid they may be watery or chalky white. In nestling diarrhoea they will be a sort of dirty cream color and of a stringy consistency.

One of the most important indications of the condition of a bird is the abdomen. The abdominal walls are so thin that changes in the underlying organs can often be detected while the bird is still alive. When the liver is enlarged, the portion of the abdomen over that organ will be puffed and the organ is likely to show through. The same thing is true when the intestines are inflamed, only in this case the abdomen has a corrugated appearance. In other cases the abdomen may be greatly enlarged or it may be shrunken and shriveled looking. It may vary in color from the light yellow of surplus fat to the deep purple of acute indigestion or the blue-black of gangrene.

The temperature of the body often indicates the state of affairs existing within it. The temperature of a normal canary in breeding condition is 107½ degrees F. That is nine degrees higher than the normal temperature of a human being. In sickness the temperature may vary from as low as 96 degrees F. to as high as 113 degrees F. And while it is not always practical to measure the temperature of a bird with a thermometer, one can usually judge if there is a fever or subnormal temperature by the action of the bird. In fever the bird will breathe more rapidly, while the subnormal bird will fluff the feathers and shiver. And here it may be pointed out that the fever is Nature's method of fighting infection. A high fever may indicate a very serious condition, but it means also that the body is putting up a fight; a subnormal temperature means that the body is whipped and has almost stopped fighting.

MY BIRD IS DEAD 149

I say almost, for the shivering is an attempt by the body to produce heat.

Now, by summarizing the observations mentioned above, we have a picture of the disease which includes history, abnormal conduct, state of droppings, the physical symptoms given by the abdomen and temperature. This is not a complete picture of the disease; but if the observations have been carefully made, they will positively identify a wide range of ailments and provide the breeder with a sound basis of facts upon which to base his treatment of the case in hand. It must, however, be remembered that symptoms can mean something to the breeder only when by study and experience he has provided himself with true pictures of the diseases to which birds are subject. For this purpose it is necessary to know what changes taking place inside of the body are responsible for the symptoms of sickness.

Pathology

Pathology is the branch of medical science that treats of the morbid changes taking place inside the body during disease. Many of these changes can be studied only with the aid of the most powerful microscopes, but there are also many that may be observed with the naked eye or a hand lens. Whenever a bird dies, the breeder should make it a rule to see how many of these changes he can find, writing them down along with the symptoms noted. He will soon learn that each set of changes has its own set of symptoms, and it is then and then only that he can begin to treat his birds intelligently.

The body should be opened carefully as soon after death as possible and the condition of each organ noted. The bird is first picked, and anything out of the ordinary on the skin is noted. The skin over the breast and abdomen is pulled away, and the condition of the breast muscles and the outer peritoneal surface noted. The peritoneum (the thin, transparent membrane covering the abdominal organs) is then opened. In health the peritoneum is thinner than the thinnest tissue paper and perfectly transparent but in disease it may be cloudy, thickened, injected with blood, or covered with a false membrane. The cavity may contain a clear fluid, a blood fluid, a thick, pasty or fibrinous exudate, or a cheesy mass; or in other cases there may be seen yellow, gray, or greenish patches covering only a portion of its surface. The breast is then divided with a pair of thin shears, or a thin, sharp knife blade, exposing the organs.

It will be impossible here to give more than a hint of all the changes that may be found by a careful naked eye examination, but the most important are classified as follows:

An organ may be anaemic—pale and bloodless; hyperaemic (engorged with blood); atrophied (shriveled up, smaller than normal); hypertrophied (enlarged or thickened); hemorrhagic (containing spots where the blood has escaped from the vessels into cavities or tissue); necrotic (containing spots where the tissue has been destroyed). Necrotic spots may be white, yellow, gray, blue, or black. And in addition to these changes there may be exudates into any of the bodily cavities or upon any of the mucous or serous surfaces. All these things can be seen by the naked eye, and many of them may be recognized the first time that they are seen; but there are many that would not be recognized unless the breeder knew how the organs looked in health. Every breeder should know that. There are

MY BIRD IS DEAD 151

enough birds killed by accidents to supply the knowledge, and all that is required to get it is to take the bodies apart and see how they look. The habit of making such examinations on all birds that die, and in the case of sickness, killing well birds for comparison, where there is doubt about whether or not the sick organs are normal, may seem to some a needless waste of time and of life; but in the long run the knowledge gained will pay large returns. And when the breeder runs into a really serious disease that threatens his whole flock, he will be able to describe it so that those he asks for advice will be able to recognize it.

CHAPTER XVI

BACTERIOLOGY

TAKING SPECIMENS

The bird should be examined as shortly after death as possible. The body should first be picked clean and dipped in a solution of disinfectant and placed on a clean glass plate. (If you have no glass plate handy a china dinner plate will do.) Then before proceeding with the examination provide yourself with the following:

A piece of number 24 chrome nickel wire—iron wire will do; so will a hat pin; a pair of tweezers; several microscopic slides or strips of window glass one inch wide and two and one-half inches long; an alcohol lamp; a pair of thin pointed embroidery shears; and a small sharp knife. If cultures are to be made, provide yourself with culture media. Several firms now put this up in sealed tubes with a sterile plug in the same box so that no making and sterilizing of media is necessary. One of these firms is the Parke Davis Co., whose media can be bought at almost any drug store or dispensary. There are dozens of different kinds, some solid and some liquid. Where a culture is to be taken and then sent to someone else for examination a solid medium should be used. The three kinds that I have found most useful are litmus-lactose agar, plain agar, and plain nutrient gelatin.

Wash the shears, knife, and pieces of glass under the water tap and then place them in a pan of boiling water on the stove. When they have been in the hot water for twenty minutes, you are ready to go on with

BACTERIOLOGY

your examination. Fish out your tweezers and with them pull the skin off the bird's abdomen and breast. With the shears split the breast so as to expose all the organs.

The first organ to examine after opening the body is the liver. The healthy liver should be a deep reddish-brown, just about the same color as fresh beef liver or somewhat lighter. Normally there should be no spots or off-color marking on it. Any that are noted are certain to be the result of pathological changes. If it is desired to send merely the liver to someone else for examination, lift it up carefully with the tweezers and with the knife cut away the connecting tissue so that it can be removed without breaking if possible. Dip the fresh liver into your burning alcohol and hold it there until it starts to turn a lighter color; then remove it and place it on one of your pieces of glass. The alcohol will draw the water out of the surface tissue and harden it. The germs in the interior of the organ may remain alive and uncontaminated for several days. The person wanting to make pure cultures of them scorches the surface of the organ with a hot wire, opens it with a sterile knife, and then proceeds as will be explained shortly. The liver with the surface dried can be wrapped in a piece of paper to protect it.

Where it is desired to take a sample of the blood or merely a small amount of tissue under sterile conditions, two of your little glass plates are taken out of the water, dried over the lamp, and permitted to cool with their faces always together. They are held together evenly and never permitted to separate for an instant. This is to prevent the inner faces from becoming contaminated with germs from your hands or the air. Then with your sterile tweezers (every time anything you are using is used or permitted to touch anything it must be placed back in the boiling water so as always to be sterile when you want to use it again) you pick up the tissue you want, place it quickly between the two glass plates, and press them together. If it is liver tissue that you want, force your sterile tweezers down into the organ as soon as it is uncovered and pull out a piece of the tissue about half the size of a match head. Place it between the plates as just described. If it is blood that you want, grasp the point of the heart with the tweezers, jerk the organ out and quickly hold it between the plates. If there is no blood dripping out of it (usually there will be), hold your wire or hat pin in the flame of your lamp for a moment; then with it press a drop of blood out of the heart and let it fall on the lower plate, dropping the other one on it quickly.

The five organs that are the most likely to contain the germs of disease are the liver, spleen, heart (or heart blood), lungs, and kidneys. Cultures from the liver, spleen, and heart blood are quite likely to be pure if carefully taken. Those from the lungs and kidneys are not so likely to be pure, as they sometimes contain bacteria that have no relation to the conditions of disease. Pure cultures can be taken from the lungs in the case of pneumonia, if the wire be inserted into the spot of the pneumonic consolidation. The healthy lung tissue is a pale pink in color. It should not be red. If it is uniformly red it means that it is inflamed, or is what is called "hyperaemic." The hyperaemic lung may in some cases look much like the pneumonic lung, but the floating test will always differentiate them. Pneumonic tissue will not float. Usually hyperaemia involves the whole lung, while in pneumonia only spots in the lung are involved. If it is contagious pneumonia and the bird has died of the disease, the spots will be thicker than the lung and bluish gray in color. This is called gray hepatization. If the bird has died of sporadic pneumonia, the spots will be a deep red, perhaps almost a liver color, thicker than the lung itself instead of thinner and looking as though the tissue had decomposed and wasted—which is just what has happened. Such spots will always give pure cultures of the germ causing the condition.

TAKING THE CULTURES

Having decided on the number of cultures to be taken, a tube is made ready for each. When the tubes are taken from the box, it will be noticed that, at about 1½ inches from the sealed end, the culture tube has been cut partly through with a diamond or glass cutter. With each culture tube is a small glass tube with a sterile cotton plug in it, the open end of which is wrapped in paper. Take off this paper wrapping but do not remove the plug from its tube. Hold the cut place on the culture tube so that the point of your flame may strike the cut. The tube will crack off evenly at the cut; and as soon as it does, the tube is rotated in the flame for a few moments; the cotton plug is removed from the tube in which it came and inserted into the open end of the culture tube, care being taken to see that the plug does not touch anything when being transferred from the one tube to the other. If the plug should touch anything it should be scorched in the flame, either before inserting it into the culture tube or afterwards, by holding the plugged end of the culture tube in the flame for a moment. The culture tube is always held by the lower or closed end; the hand should never touch it within less than two inches from the plugged end. As the tubes are broken and plugged they may be set up in an empty teacup until you are ready to inoculate them.

Before the inoculation it is best to label each tube with the date, the number of the bird, and the organ from which it is to be inoculated. This is all done before the bird is opened as a rule, but it is a good plan to have several other tubes handy so that in case you find things that you were not looking for and desire to make other cultures you may have the tubes in readiness.

Now open the bird, first exposing the liver. Run your wire through the flame until every part of it from the point back five or six inches has been heated to redness. Pick up the liver tube in one hand, holding the open end away from your body; thrust the point of your sterile wire into the liver and twist it around so as to pick up some of the blood and cells in it. Then with the second and third finger of the same hand that is holding the wire you quickly remove the plug from the culture tube and thrust the wire down into the medium clear to the bottom of the tube and as quickly remove the wire, replace the plug, and again hold the plugged end of the tube in the flame for a moment. Reflame your wire before laying it down.

The spleen is the next organ to examine. In order to do this it must be exposed and uncovered by removing the liver. As soon as the liver is removed a small flesh-colored organ will be seen. Its position is under the upper edge of the left lobe of the liver. The organ is shaped like a banana and normally in the canary is about 1-16 of an inch in diameter and 3-16 to 5-16 of an inch long. In disease it may be enlarged until it is from 1-8 to 3-16 of an inch in diameter and 7-8 of an inch long. Little is known about the functions of this

BACTERIOLOGY 157

organ in any animal, but that it has an important place in the body's defenses against disease is very likely. It may also have something to do with the digestive processes in birds; for in the canary there are two tubes connecting the spleen to the proventriculus (the glandular stomach just above the gizzard). After the spleen is located and its size and condition noted cultures may be made from it just as in the case of the liver. Inasmuch as the organ is so small, and normally so tough, but at the same time flexible, it is often necessary to pick it up with sterile tweezers in order to hold it in such a way that the flamed needle can be thrust into it.

Next uncover the heart by splitting the breast. It will be noted that there are two little sacs at the top of the heart. These are the auricles into which the blood collects from the veins before going into the pumping chambers (ventricles) to be forced out into the arteries. Not always, but very often, these auricles are found upon examination to be full of blood, and it is very easy to thrust a wire into them to inoculate the cultures. These cultures are to be marked "Heart Blood." When they produce growths of the organism causing the disease, it is proof that the disease is septicemic in nature.

In many cases there will be found exudates in the pericardium (heart sac) or necrotic spots in the walls of the heart itself, and it may be desirable to make cultures of these portions, which should be carefully marked so as to distinguish them from those made from the heart blood.

At the time the heart was uncovered, the lungs were also exposed. Pneumonic or necrotic spots in the lungs can usually be seen without removing them, and it is best to make the cultures before the lungs are touched. It may, and often does happen, that when the auricle is punctured the blood will run out over the lungs. This is, however, easily removed by dipping the body into the solution of disinfectant that should always be handy when making an examination of a body.

The kidneys are dark greyish brown organs that fit into concavities in the ilium (the bone that carries the hip joints), one on each side of the spine. Each kidney in a bird has three lobes. The blood vessel and ureters are plainly visible on the surface as exposed after removing the gizzard and intestines. Sometimes in disease, only one kidney or one lobe of one kidney, will be enlarged or discolored; at other times both kidneys and all three lobes of each will be equally affected. The cultures are made from the kidneys in the same way as in the case of the other organs, but it is not necessary or wise to remove them for the purpose.

As soon as the cultures are made, wash your hands in disinfectant solution. Reflame the open end of each tube and wrap a piece of paper over it, holding the paper in place with a rubber band. If the cultures are to be sent to a laboratory for examination the tubes can be packed right back into the boxes in which they came, the ends of the boxes bent over and tied with string. All should be tied together and a letter placed with them explaining all that is known about the disease causing the death of the bird, all notes taken during the examination, together with a request that any pathogenic organism found shall be classified and identified if possible. The letter or note should be placed right with the culture and the package wrapped and shipped at once by first class mail or by express (it is against the law to send a package containing a letter by parcel post). If the breeder wants to incubate his own cultures, he may do so by placing the tubes in a warm dark place for a few days. They should be inspected in a good-light every six hours. The gelatin tubes should be kept in a warm place in the room; it must not be too hot or the gelatin will melt; but, the cultures will stand a temperature of 70 to 75 degrees F. The agar tubes should be kept as near blood heat as possible. In from 24 to 72 hours, as a rule, changes will be noticed inside of the tube, and it is often the nature of the changes that identifies the germs present.

BLOOD CULTURES

It is often desirable to know what kind of germs a bird has in his blood and how many, while he is still alive; and to get this information blood cultures are made. It is not an easy or safe job to draw blood from a vein of a canary during life without harming him, so I prefer to draw it from one of his toes. The tubes are broken and plugged the same as before, but this time three tubes are used. The medium is either plain agar or plain gelatin, but instead of putting them into an empty teacup they are placed first in boiling water until the medium melts and then into the cup filled with hot water, so as to keep them warm.

The bird is caught and one of his feet washed with warm water, soap, and a soft brush. Wash well around the claws, then paint the nail on one of his toes with tincture of iodine, taking care not to get any of the iodine on his damp foot. (It might blister.) He is wrapped in a piece of bandage so that the cleaned foot is left sticking out and cannot come in contact with anything. One toe nail is clipped with a pair of sterile shears, making the cut exactly at the end of the vein. The small drop of blood that will ooze out is caught on the wire, which for this purpose should have had the end bent around a number 18 wire so as to form a loop.

The looped wire is run through the flame as the blood is oozing out; and when there is a drop on the end of the toe big enough to fill the loop, it is picked up with the flamed loop and transferred to the first tube which should now be cooled to about 110 degrees F., that is, it should feel fairly warm to the hand but not hot. After stirring the medium in the tube well with the loop, the loop is removed and flamed. The tube is also flamed just as before. Then this first tube and one of the others are picked up in the hand together. The plugs are removed from both at once and are held so that they do not touch anything. With the flamed loop one loopful of the medium in tube number one is transferred to tube number two. The plugs are put in and the tubes and wire flamed again. Then a loopful of medium is transferred in the same manner from tube number two to tube number three. Now the tubes are placed in cold water to harden the media. If agar is used they are placed in a slanting position so that the medium will run up one side of the tube; if gelatin is used the tubes are held in this position and rotated or twirled about as they are cooling. The gelatin will cool in a thin layer on the sides of the tube and thus permit the colonies to be seen very easily. When cooling the tubes, care must be taken that the medium does not touch the plug on the inside and that the water does not touch it on the outside. The tubes should be placed in a warm place to incubate.

If the bird has very few germs in his blood, there will be few colonies in the first tube and maybe none at all in the second and third tubes; but where there are many germs in the blood, there may be so many colonies in the first tube that they cannot be counted. In such cases, it is possible by computing the amount of medium in the tube and the amount that the loop will hold to estimate fairly accurately how many germs there are in each cubic centimeter of blood. This is, however, a process requiring different equipment and a more complicated procedure, but, then, the calculation is not necessary in order to get the information desired. A mere comparison of the tubes taken on successive days will often make certain whether the germs in the blood are increasing or decreasing in number, and that is what one wants to know.

The method just described is a very good one for isolating different strains of germs when more than one kind is present, or when there is contamination; since in the third tube there will be in such event few colonies, far apart, each one due to a single germ, and pure. If the germs are of different kinds, the colonies will be different, and by bending the end of your wire into an "L", you can stick it into the tube and one at a time inoculate new tubes from each of the different colonies, flaming the wire each time, of course.

Where a course of treatments is being used to remove the germs from the blood, the blood cultures will tell you just how long it takes to bring about the desired result. This method just described is the one that I have used in testing the reactions to Stroud's Specific.

CHAPTER XVII

SOME ORGANISMS PATHOGENIC TO BIRDS
BACTERIUM PASTEURELLA AVIUM
The Germ of Fowl Cholera

This germ was described in 1886 by Flugge, who gave it the name *Bacillus Cholerae-Gallinarum.* It has also been called *B. Bipolaris Septicus* and *B. Avicida.*

This germ besides being the cause of disease in poultry is often found in the blood of canaries suffering with septic fever (diphtheria). It is the cause of a disease in canaries which has the same symptoms as cholera in poultry and which I have described elsewhere under the heading "Hemorrhagic Septicemia."

The organism is a small oval rod from .4 to .6 microns wide and one to two microns long, (A micron is 1/1000 of a millimeter and is the unit of measurement used for bacteria) or about 1/50,000 of an inch wide and from 1/25,000 to 1/12,000 of an inch long. To obtain an adequate idea of the minute size of these germs it may be said that a red corpuscle, which must be magnified 100 times in order to be visible, has a diameter 12 times the length of the germs in question. The organism has no power of motion of its own and does not form spores. It stains with aniline dyes, and in smears from tissue it takes the stain more heavily at the ends than in the center of the organism. This is called bipolar staining.

B. Pasteurella can be grown on agar, and after 48 hours at incubator temperature, 98 degrees F., or about three days in an ordinarily warm room, colonies appear. They are round, smooth, shiny discs that look gray by reflected light and muddy brown by transmitted light.

PATHOGENIC ORGANISMS

The colonies below the surface are round and bean-shaped.

On gelatin at room temperature (about 70 degrees F.) the organism grows very slowly; it takes from one to two weeks for the colonies to become visible to the naked eye. Those on the surface appear like small raised dots no larger than the head of a pin. When looked at by transmitted light each dot acts like a tiny lens and shows a bright point of light in its center. In stab cultures the growth extends along the entire length of the needle path and is composed of a great number of small distinct colonies. The surface growth is round and gray in color, and does not as a rule extend to the sides of the tube.

In sugar-free alkaline bouillon there is a slight cloudiness after the lapse of two or three days. The reaction as the culture becomes old remains alkaline. In bouillon containing glucose, saccharose, or muscle sugar, the reaction becomes acid after a period of two days. Bouillon containing lactose remains alkaline in reaction. In sugar bouillon there will usually be a sediment in the bottom of the tube and a blue ring around the wall of the tube at the surface of the medium. There is no pellicle (floating scum) on the surface of liquid media.

STREPTOCOCCUS OF APOPLECTIFORM SEPTICEMIA

This germ was described by Norgaard and Mohler, Bureau of Animal Industry, in 1902.

Cocci are small round organisms and the streptococci are those that form themselves into chains. The coccus in question is about six tenths of a micron in diameter. It stains with the ordinary aniline dyes and retains the stain when first treated with iodine and then washed in alcohol according to a process developed by Gram. Germs that retain the color when treated by this process are called Gram positive; those that do not are called Gram negative.

In alkaline bouillon growth appears within 24 hours. The medium becomes stringy and cloudy and there is a deposit on the sides and bottom of the tube. If the tube is examined carefully, fine web-like strings may sometimes be seen hanging from the sides of the tube. After several days, the growth settles to the bottom of the tube, forming a white sediment which breaks up into small particles when the tube is twirled between the palms of the hands.

On agar, the growth appears within 24 to 48 hours as small shiny gray colonies that reach a size of 1.5 mm in diameter on the third or fourth day. They appear under transmitted light brown in color with pearly-blue borders. Colonies below the surface appear as minute pearly-blue points. In stab cultures there is little or no growth on the surface, but along the entire needle path there is a mass of very small grayish white colonies with loop-like (fimbriated borders) wavy outgrowths into the media. The organism studied by me in fits in canaries differed from those here described in that the surface colonies did not show any brown under transmitted light but were a pearly-blue even when several weeks old. They did not attain a size greater than .7 mm., (a little larger than a maw seed) and looked like small drops of dew.

In gelatin stab cultures there may be a slight growth on the fourth or fifth day, appearing along the needle path, but there is no growth on the surface. The canary strain made visible growth on only about one gelatin tube out of four and then the growth was very slight. In all other respects this germ appeared identical with the one described for the poultry disease.

In bouillon containing sugar, the growth is much heavier than on sugar-free media, and the reaction becomes strongly acid. There is, however, no formation of gas. Litmus-lactose agar is a good medium for growing this organism, and the colonies will show the acid formation by their reddish coloring.[10]

BACTERIUM SANGUINARIUM
The Germ of Fowl Typhoid

This germ was first discovered in England in 1889 by Klein and given the name *Bacillus Gallinarum*. In 1895 it was found in the United States by Moore and given the name used here.

This organism which is a small Gram negative rod about one micron in diameter and about 1.5 microns long, sometimes appears nearly spherical in shape. It stains with the ordinary aniline dyes.

"The organism is obtained in pure cultures from the heart blood or liver of birds dead from the disease, and is readily cultivated on ordinary media.

"Agar. On this medium at 37 degrees C. the growth is moderately vigorous, having a grayish glistening appearance. Isolated colonies are from one to two mm. in diameter, convex, and with sharply defined borders. Agar plates emit a peculiar penetrating odor, which differs decidedly from the pungent odor given off by *Bacterium suisepticum*. The growth on this medium resembles very closely that of *B. suipestifer*.

"Gelatin. In this medium the growth is less vigorous. In stick cultures it is more abundant along the line

---

[10] I believe that this same germ is responsible for the paralytic disease of parrots and parrakeets, although I have not had a chance to study those diseases myself.

of inoculation than on the surface. Isolated colonies are about 0.25 mm. in diameter, appearing to the unaided eye as homogeneous bodies. There is no liquefaction or softening of the medium.

"Potato. On the surface of potato a delicate grayish-yellow growth appears after forty-eight hours when kept at 35 degrees C. Frequently there is no development owing, presumably, to the acid in the potato.

"Bouillon. In alkaline bouillon at 36 degrees C. the growth imparts a uniform cloudiness to the liquid within twenty-four hours. If the bouillon contains much sugar the reaction becomes acid, otherwise it remains alkaline. A grayish friable sediment forms at the bottom of the tube. After several days the growth settles, leaving a clear supernatant fluid.

"Alkaline bouillon containing 1 percent dextrose in the fermentation tube becomes cloudy within twenty-four hours and strongly acid in reaction. Similar tubes containing saccharose and lactose become clouded throughout, but they remain alkaline in reaction. The degree of alkalinity increases with age. Gas is not produced during the growth in bouillon containing these sugars.

"Resistance. It (the germ) is destroyed at 50 degrees C. in fifteen minutes. A 1 percent solution of carbolic acid was fatal to it in five minutes. It resists drying when in films on cover-glasses for from 7 to 15 days."

This germ is not known to cause disease in birds or animals other than poultry, but I have had reason to suspect it in some outbreaks in canaries.

B. PARATYPHOSUS B.

B. Paratyphosus B. is a member of the hog cholera group of organisms which are also known as the food poisoning bacteria. It is responsible for a long list of diseases on its own account and also acts as a secondary invader in several serious diseases due to other causes. There are a great many strains that cannot be distinguished one from the other except by their pathogenic and serological characters. In appearance and cultural characteristics they are identical.

Morphology. *B. Paratyphosus B.* is a short, plump rod varying considerably in size in different strains and also varying in size according to the medium upon which it is grown. The smallest are about 5 tenths of a micron wide and 1.2 microns long. The largest (and those from the canary are among the largest) may be one micron or more in width and sometimes as many as four microns long. The organism is active, mobile, and has from three to five flagella which average about seven microns in length although some much longer are sometimes found.

It is Gram negative; stains with the aniline dyes ordinarily used. Specimens from cultures usually stain evenly, while those from tissue often exhibit a light center or bipolar staining.

On slant agar the growth is a grayish glistening, non-viscid mass. If there are isolated colonies they are convex and about the size of a rape seed or a little larger. The edges are sharp and even. In stab cultures there is a grayish line along the needle path with a vigorous growth on the surface.

On gelatin the growth is not so vigorous as on agar. The colonies appear as gray dots and do not spread unless the reaction is rather alkaline. This organism does not liquefy gelatin.

On potato, if a growth appears, it is a thin pale

yellow, glistening layer. There is no growth if the potato is strongly acid.

In alkaline bouillon it produces uniform cloudiness after 24 hours. There is as a rule no membrane on the surface. Later the growth settles and forms a grayish sediment that breaks up into fine particles when the tube is twirled between the palms of the hands. If there is muscle sugar in the bouillon, the reaction becomes first acid and later strongly alkaline. In peptonized bouillon containing dextrose, gas is formed, but no gas is developed in bouillon containing lactose and saccharose.

The reaction on milk is very characteristic and is one of the tests used to identify bacteria belonging to this group. There is no precipitation or coagulation of the milk, but the reaction becomes strongly alkaline and the alkali seems to act on or with the fats of the milk, saponifying them. The milk after several weeks becomes opalescent and later clear. If kept longer it becomes thick, due to evaporation, and turns brown.

This organism can be grown at room temperature (about 70 degrees F.) but grows best at blood heat. It is destroyed by a temperature of 60 degrees C. for ten minutes.

B. Paratyphosus B. is credited with being the cause of paratyphoid in human beings. It has been found in the intestinal tract of perfectly healthy human beings, in the intestines of healthy hogs, and it has been found in the blood of both human beings and hogs dead from a septicemic infection. It has been found associated with outbreaks of septic fever in canaries, and of psittacosis in parrots and parrakeets. It has been reported as the cause of a fatal septicemia of pigeons known as "Megrims" in which there occurs inflammation of the

PATHOGENIC ORGANISMS

brain with a friable exudate in the subarachnoid space over the cerebellum and the posterior lobes of the cerebrum. (The exudate is grayish yellow in color and is easily removed. The brain tissue under the exudate is reddish in color. This germ has also been reported as the cause of a disease of pigeons that can be distinguished with difficulty from Avian Diphtheria. It causes fatal septicemia in mice and rats. It is responsible for a fatal septicemia of canaries that has the following symptoms and morbid anatomy:

Symptoms

In the beginning the bird carriers the feathers fluffed out and sleeps a good deal, but eats and drinks as usual, seeming not to be seriously sick. As the disease progresses the bird stops eating and sits with its eyes half closed. The breathing becomes very rapid. The bird gets weak and moves about with difficulty, then becomes unconscious and dies in a convulsion.

Morbid Anatomy

The legs are extended from the body and stiffen quickly after death. The intestines are inflamed and thickened; the spleen shows hyperaemic enlargement and may be from two to five times the normal size; the liver and kidneys are also apt to be enlarged and hyperaemic. An organism that cannot be differentiated from B. Paratyphosus B. of human origin is always obtainable in pure cultures from the blood and organs of birds that have died from this disease.

Treatment

Five grains of sulphate of iron to the quart of drinking water has been recommended as a treatment for this malady. It may be promptly cured by the use of Stroud's Specific by mixing the antiseptic and salts in equal parts and adding one teaspoonful to each quart of water.

Where this treatment is unavailable I would suggest that citro-carbonate (see formula) be mixed with equal parts of Glauber's salt and one teaspoonful of the mixture be added to each quart of drinking water; then, after the mixture stops foaming, add one ounce of peroxide of hydrogen solution. Give this mixture to the bird for drinking water. Do not give it in anything but glass drinkers.

This disease is in many respects very similar to the gastro-enteritic form of apoplectiform septicemia, both in symptoms, morbid anatomy, and treatment. Also in apoplectiform septicemia the source of the disease must be looked for in stale food and water where the infection is sporadic. There are some cases where the germ may attain a virulence sufficient to cause a direct contagion. When this happens the disease is very serious and is liable to cause the death of all birds in the aviary in a few days. Such contagions are almost always brought into the bird room with newly purchased birds. All new birds should be quarantined, and wherever a contagious disease shows itself, the prophylactic measures recommended for septic fever should be resorted to at once.

ORGANISM OF INFECTIOUS NECROSIS
Bacillus Canariensis Necrophorus

This organism is a member of the Pasteurella or hemorrhagic septicemia group and differs from the germ of fowl cholera in pathogenicity and also in so far as it is slightly larger in size, and that the colonies on agar are smaller and slightly more granular.

The germ of fowl cholera will produce disease in

PATHOGENIC ORGANISMS 171

practically the same experimental animals, but the canary organism is reported to be unable to produce disease in hens. The lesions caused by the two germs in the canary are distinctly different in nature.

Freese Disease

Freese has described septicemia disease of canaries due to a germ having the following characteristics:

It is a small rod 0.5 to 1.5 microns long which stains uniformly with aniline dyes. The organism is always found in the heart blood of birds that have died from the disease to which it gives rise, but it is detected with difficulty in the organs of birds that have recently died, although in bodies that have lain for several hours the bacteria are very plentiful. It grows best in the air but can grow anaerobically (without oxygen).

On agar the colonies appear within 12 hours if the cultures are kept at blood heat. Such colonies are about the size of a maw seed, and have a bright, shiny appearance, raised centers, becoming uniformly thinner toward the edges. They have a light gray color under reflected light and bright blue by transmitted light. The colonies very much resemble fine dew drops and will develop at room temperature (about 70° F.) but the growth is slower.

On gelatin the colonies do not appear until the second day and then as fine gray-white points that show a brown center by transmitted light. Shortly thereafter a bright transparent area forms around each colony showing the beginning of liquefaction. Five days from the time the culture was seeded the whole plate is liquefied.

In bouillon at blood heat there is uniform cloudiness after 14 hours and the formation of a viscous sediment. After five days the cloudiness begins to disappear from the upper part of the tube and after fourteen days the liquid becomes entirely clear. There is a thick brownish-gray sediment in the bottom of the tube. No pellicle is formed.

On potato the growth appears in 18 hours. The colonies are prominent, sharply outlined, about the size of a maw seed, and gray-white. The growth forms a uniform layer along the needle path.

Milk is coagulated in 15 hours at blood heat and in 32 hours at room temperature. There is formation of lactic acid in milk, but neither acid nor gas is formed in sugar media.

The organism will cause death in canaries, sparrows, and mice, but not in hens, pigeons, rabbits, and guinea pigs.

Symptoms in the Canary

On the first day the bird is less lively than usual and carries its feathers loosely. On the second day it is puffed up most of the time but continues to eat and drinks more than usual. It breathes a little faster than normal at this time. There may be some diarrhoea. It is characteristic of this disease that the bird leaves the perch frequently and moves around like a well bird, but as the disease progresses these moments of activity becomes less frequent, and toward the last the bird sits at the bottom of the cage with its head turned back into the feathers. At this time the breathing is shallow and very rapid. The bird continues to eat up to within a few hours of death.

Morbid Anatomy

The upper intestines are red and swollen. The liver may be very much congested and enlarged or it may be yellow and have the structure destroyed to the extent

PATHOGENIC ORGANISMS

that it breaks up easily. There are usually no changes in the spleen, although once in a while this organ may be slightly enlarged.

Treatment

Having had no experience with this disease myself, no treatment can be recommended outside of the general treatments that have proven effective in other diseases of a septicemic nature.

Freese remarks that among the organisms grown on media there are many forms that might be mistaken for a diplococcus.

ORGANISM OF SPORADIC PNEUMONIA IN CANARIES

In several cases of sporadic pneumonia in canaries I found an organism quite similar to the one just described.

On agar the growth was rather moderately fleshy along the needle path, and just above the condensation water, extending about half way to the side of the tube. The dew-like colonies mentioned above were not noted. In plate cultures, or tube cultures seeded into melted agar, the colonies below the surface were small gray points, some of them seeming to have a fleck of brown in the center.

On gelatin the growth was identical with that above described so far as the description goes, but in the cultures studied by me it was noteworthy that after the medium was completely liquefied a large lumpy mass collected in the bottom of the tube. This mass did not break up and settle uniformly over the bottom of the tube, but remained clumped and half suspended in the liquid, merely touching the bottom lightly.

On potato there are gray colonies just like those described by Freese, but there is also a diffused gray growth extending into the body of the potato way through the plug. The growth on potato is rather dry.

Unfortunately I was not able to do my own microscopic work and have to trust the reports of others on this organism. The report that I received from the microscopist to whom I submitted cultures and organs was that the germ was a Gram positive staphlococcus closely resembling the *Staphlococcus Pyogenes Aureus*. In cultural characteristics it has many points of similarity with the pus germ but little or no pigment was formed.

Symptoms

The bird puffs up his feathers suddenly and starts sleeping in the day time. He will wake up and drink occasionally the first day but usually makes no effort to eat. After moving around for a moment or two he will hop up on the perch and go to sleep again. There is at first no fast breathing or great weakness. The bird sleeps on one foot the first day; the second day he seems weaker and neither eats nor drinks. He may still be sleeping on one foot, however, until along in the afternoon when he will be on two feet, and usually by night he will be down at the bottom of the cage. Very seldom does he live until the morning of the third day. The droppings are very scanty and are of a reddish-brown color that is very characteristic of the disease. There is no white whatever on the dropping and there appears to be no action of the kidneys.

Morbid Anatomy

The liver and kidneys may be slightly enlarged; the spleen is normal; the principal changes are in the lungs, where in one or both will be found red spots extending clear through the lung. There may be one or several spots in the single lung and they may vary in

PATHOGENIC ORGANISMS

size from mere points to spots ¼ inch in diameter. When cut out they do not float in water. They extend through the lung from front to back, and the spot is thinner than the tissue itself.

From the heart blood and pneumonic spots always, and from the liver, kidneys, and spleen, but less often, pure cultures of the organism mentioned above can be obtained; but in many cases where the duration of the disease has been very short, the cultures from the liver, spleen, and kidneys will be sterile.

Treatment

This is a very difficult disease to treat because it is sporadic in nature running a very short course; and as only one bird at a time is infected, there is little chance for making a diagnosis before the opportunity for treatment has passed. In this respect it is very much like lobar pneumonia in human beings. In a large number of cases having the symptoms of this disease in which the birds were given Avian Antiseptic in solution with honey, dropped into the beak, there was rapid recovery.

This solution is made up by adding to one half teaspoonful of honey enough warm water to make up one ounce and by then adding to this two grains of the antiseptic. The solution should be drawn up into a medicine dropper or syringe. The bird must be held gently but firmly in one hand with the forefinger of that hand held out alongside his head to prevent it from being turned away from the operator and to keep it level. The opening of the dropper or the point of the needle should not be forced into the mouth but should be held at the junction of the upper and lower mandibles, thus permitting the fluid to run in very slowly. It is possible by this method and the use of a great deal of patience to get the bird to swallow a considerable amount of the medicine. I always give it all that I can get it to take this way at a single dose; and where a cure is effected, the single dose is usually enough to bring it about. I have not found repeated doses of much value in this ailment.

BACILLUS COLI

Bacillus Coli is a natural inhabitant of the intestines of all species of animals, man not excepted, and also of the intestines of all birds. Apart from this it is found only in milk, water, and soil that have been contaminated by excrement. It is not the specific cause of any disease, but has often been found associated with various diseases in both man and animals: but while this germ is ordinarly not pathogenic, some strains of the organism seem to possess or acquire the power to cause disease under conditions that are not well understood but which are quite likely due to causes that lower the normal resistance of the host. Numerous outbreaks of fatal septicemia in fowls due to *B. Coli* have been reported by a number of investigators. The germs have also been discovered in canaries, pigeons, pheasants, quail, grouse, and certain other birds. A great many strains of this organism have been found to be pathogenic for the canary, and much of the disease that follows long shipments is probably due to the invasion of the body by this organism while the resistance is low.

The symptoms and lesions reported for the various outbreaks of disease due to this organism differ widely, one from the other, but each outbreak is reported as showing constant lesions throughout its course. Most of the outbreaks have cholera-like symptoms. There may be pneumonia, peritonitis, necrotic changes in the liver, spleen, or kidneys, or the disease may cause no other changes than those common to purely septicemic infections.

While there is an unlimited number of strains of *B. Coli* showing minor differences, there are just two well defined varieties. The first, which is known as variety A will form gas in dextrose, lactose, and saccharose. The second, known as variety B, or *B. Coli communior* (because it is thought to be the more common variety), does not form gas in saccharose.

B. Coli is a small oval rod. There is considerable variation in size between different strains and in addition to variations due to the medium upon which the germs are grown. *B. Coli* is usually from 0.4 to 0.7 of a micron wide and one to three microns long. It is motile and may have from one to as many as 7 flagella. It stains with the ordinary dyes, sometimes showing bipolar staining, and is Gram negative. It grows well on all the usual media, and while it develops best at blood heat, it can be grown without difficulty at room temperature, (about 70° F.).

Agar. The surface colonies on this medium are mostly round, though where they are close together they may coalesce to form odd shapes, but always with the borders composed of convex curves. The growth is gray-white and rather opaque except near the edges where it usually shows a pearly-blue iridescence by transmitted light. The colonies below the surface are small, gray, and likely to have outgrowths extending into the surrounding medium.

Gelatin. On this medium the colonies appear in from 18 to 36 hours. Those deep in the interior of the medium are round, oval, or whetstone shaped, of yellow color, rarely more than one mm. in diameter. The surface colonies appear as small, flat, irregular, blue-white points, some colonies having outgrowths from the edges. Stab cultures take the nail form, the surface growth usually, but not always, reaching to the sides of the tube. Gelatin is not liquefied.

Potato. The growth on this medium is very characteristic at times, but in order to assure a characteristic growth, it is a good plan to let a drop or two of 1/10 normal sodium hydroxide fall upon the potato plug before it is sterilized in order to forestall any anticipated acid reaction.

The growth appears within 24 to 36 hours at blood heat and usually within 48 hours at about 70 degrees F. It is a thick, moist, yellow, brownish, or cream colored deposit that usually covers most of the surface of the plug. It often resembles pus in appearance and where several strokes have been made with the needle there may be a sort of bubbling up of the growth which makes the needle path discernible.

Bouillon. In this medium there is produced a heavy diffused cloudiness, sediment, and occasionally a slight surface growth. If sugar is present both acid and a large amount of gas are formed. In dextrose and lactose fermentation tubes, the gas will fill half of the closed branch and will be composed of one part carbon dioxide and two part hydrogen.

Variety A ferments saccharose; the gas formed, filling about two-thirds of the closed branch of the tube, is composed of two parts carbon dioxide and three parts hydrogen.

Variety B does not ferment saccharose and the reaction remains alkaline.

Milk is rendered acid and the casein is coagulated. The curd is compact and solid, much of it being soluble in alkalies with difficulty, if not actually insoluble.

PATHOGENIC ORGANISMS 179

The bodies of *B. Coli* contain a poison that is not in the media but which will cause serious symptoms when the dead cells are injected into animals.

Note: In 1930 the body of an imported Yorkshire was sent to me for examination. This was one of a large number of birds that had become sick shortly after arriving in this country. The disease was thought to be septic fever, but the body displayed none of the lesions of that disease. A strain of variety A *B. Coli* was obtained in pure culture from all of the organs. A drop of bouillon culture, 48 hours old, the size of a rape seed, injected under the skin on the abdomen of a canary would cause death in three to four days. The principal lesions were necrotic spots in the liver. In some cases there was a general peritonitis. The organism was obtained in pure culture from the organs and blood of the bird that had died from the disease. Inoculated birds did not transmit the disease to healthy birds caged with them. As the disease reported to me had been very contagious I concluded at the time that the germ found was a post-mortem invader that happened to possess some virulence. The original disease as well as the inoculated disease was promptly cured by the use of Stroud's Specific.

CHAPTER XVIII

DRUGS

List With Notes on Their Mixtures and Use

Acetic Acid. This is the acid principle of vinegar. It comes in many degrees of intensity. Chemical formula is CH_3COOH. It is soluble in water and alcohol in all proportions.

Glacial Acetic Acid is a very caustic liquid with a sharp, acid odor containing $99\frac{1}{2}\%$ of CH_3COOH. It has been recommended as a treatment for a mould infection of the skin of birds that is sometimes called fungoid skin. As this acid is very caustic it should be used with the utmost care. I do not recommend the use of it until other remedies have been tried ineffectively. Where it seems necessary it should be applied with a small brush to the infected part and to only a small area at a time. Of course, it should not be allowed to get into the bird's eyes.

Dilute Acetic Acid. This is a pure form of vinegar and contains 6% CH_3COOH. It is used as an appetizer, diuretic, and anti-fat. It is of use in treating birds that are suffering with liver trouble due to overfeeding. The dose is from 5 to 15 drops in each ounce of drinking water given in glass containers.

Benzoic Acid. Sometimes called flour of benzoin, is obtained from the hardened sap and resin of the *styrax benzoini,* a Peruvian tree, by sublimation. The chemical formula is C_6H_5COOH. It comes as white or faintly yellow pearly plates or needles of an agreeable, aromatic odor and taste. It is soluble in 281 parts of water at 25 degrees C. or at the temperature of a fairly warm room and is very soluble in alcohol. The solubility in water is increased by adding a pinch of sodium phosphate to the water. This acid evaporates without melting at the temperature of boiling water. It is an ingredient of *Friar's balsam, Turkington's balsam* and *Jesuit's drops,* as well as a number of other remedies. It is present in balsam of Peru and balsam of Tolu. Benzoic acid is the oldest antiseptic known.

Benzoic Acid is used externally as an antiseptic for the skin, but its principal use is as an antiseptic for the lungs and the kidneys. It has the power of regulating the acid condition of the urine, making it more or less acid as the situation may require in order to keep it in normal condition. Benzoic Acid is, therefore, often used to influence the reaction of the urine in order to make the action of other drugs possible. It also lowers the temperature in fevers. It is sometimes of value in sickness following chilling of the bird, or in colds where the bird shows some fever. Dose for a canary would be 1/16 to ¼ grain to the ounce of drinking water given always in glass vessels.

Boric Acid. This is a weak mineral acid obtained by the action of stronger acids upon borax, the chemical formula of which is H_3BO_3. It is found on the market in the form of colorless crystals or white powder with a faint bitterish-acid taste. This powder is soluble in 18 parts of water at room temperature and in 4.3 parts of boiling water, and is slightly more soluble in alcohol than in water.

Boric Acid is a mild antiseptic and is used principally in 1 to 4% solution as an eye wash. The pure powder may be used as a wound dressing, and on account of its relatively weak effect it is often used on birds where merely a mild antiseptic is required.

Carbolic Acid, Phenol. This acid is obtained from

coal-tar by fractional distillation, and may be purchased in the form of colorless crystals that draw water from the air and become liquid. It is very poisonous, highly caustic, an antiseptic, disinfectant, and insecticide. Its Chemical formula is C_6H_5OH.

Carbolic acid may be used to wash cages in a 1 or 2% solution. It is sometimes used mixed with oils to render wood work "louse-proof" and to stop the breeding of red mites. Most breeders, however, prefer cresol for this purpose, inasmuch as the latter is stronger and less poisonous. It is also cheaper than carbolic acid. 1% carbolated vasoline is about the best treatment known for Scaly-Leg, an infection of the feet due to a very small mite that eats the tissue underneath the scales.

Citric Acid. This is an organic acid from limes and lemons, which is purchasable in the form of colorless granulated crystals, or white powder. It contains one molecule of water of crystallization, is very acid in taste, permanent in cool, dry air, but effloresces in warm and deliquesces (absorbs water from the air and melts) in moist air. It is soluble in water in all proportions, and is a rather powerful antiseptic, non-poisonous and antipyretic, that is, has the power to reduce fevers. Its chemical formula is $C_3H_4(OH)(COOH)_3(H_2O)$.

Citric acid is used externally as a treatment for skin infections, internally as a diuretic, antipyretic, antiseptic and anti-fat. It is oxidized within the body and is not excreted. Citric acid is a wonderful tonic for birds that are overfat and cannot be brought into breeding condition, inasmuch as it reduces the fat and stimulates the excretion of waste matter, in this way purifying and cooling the blood. It has long been used in the treatment of diphtheria in human beings and is of great value in the treatment of diphtheria (Septic Fever) as well as all

DRUGS

fevers in birds. It is a most valuable substance in the treatment of disease but one that is more often used in mixtures with other substances as will be described later. Citric acid is one of the ingredients of my specific treatment of septic fever. The dose for a canary is about 1 grain to the ounce of drinking water given to the bird in glass vessels. In other containers, especially those of metal, highly poisonous compounds might be produced.

Citrocarbonate. There is no chemical compound by this name; but when one part by weight of citric acid is mixed with two parts by weight of sodium bicarbonate, the mixture becomes moist and very cold, and bubbles of carbon dioxide are given off. If this moist, doughy mixture is dried in a warming oven, crushed into a powder, and placed in tight jars, it will keep indefinitely.

This mixture is widely used as an antiacid in cases of indigestion and acid stomach. It is also of considerable value as a corrective for an acid condition of the blood either in fevers or in cases of rheumatism. This is one of the best and most convenient ways of giving citric acid. When a teaspoonful of this mixture is placed in a quart of water it effervesces and forms a bubbling, sparkling, drink with a pleasant lemon-like taste. As an antifat, in cases of fevers, and as a "pep-me-up" for overfed birds, the solution just described is given as drinking water. It is also of value in stopping soft moult and in reducing the size of the liver and of swollen feet in birds suffering from the effects of overfeeding. I have given this mixture (either alone or in conjunction with other laxative and diuretic salts) every day for three months without harming the birds except by causing loss of weight.

Oxalic Acid. This is an organic acid made from sawdust, whose chemical formula is $(COOH)_2$ plus $2H_2O$. It is found on the market in the form of transparent, colorless crystals soluble in water and having a very acid taste. This acid is sometimes used in human medicine, but as it is very poisonous, (killing its victim by asphyxiation) it is best not given to birds internally. It is included here because two teaspoonfuls of the crystals added to a quart of water make an excellent solution for cleaning glassware. Drinkers can be permitted to soak in the solution for an hour or two and when they are taken out and rinsed in running water all scum and deposits are removed. The glass comes out clean and sparkling and is sterile as far as disease producing bacteria are concerned.

The container of this substance should be labeled, *Poison.* Antidote: calcium, saccharate, chalk, lime water in large quantities. It may be added that in event of accidental poisoning where other substances are promptly available several teaspoonsful of ground cuttle-bone or your bird's mineral food might save you from a very dangerous situation, as this acid has a strong affinity for calcium and is neutralized by it.

Salicylic Acid. This acid whose chemical formula is $C_6H_4(CH)(COOH)$ (1:2) is obtained chemically from carbolic acid, sodium hydroxide (Lye) and carbondioxide, and is purchasable as a fine white crystaline powder, having a sweet taste with an acid after-taste. It is soluble in 308 parts of water at room temperature (about 70° F.).

This acid is an antiseptic, antirheumatic, and antipyretic. It is largely used as a specific for inflammatory rheumatism, to reduce fevers and as an intestinal antiseptic. It has been recommended for birds in cases of chronic inflammation of the bowels and indigestion. It is of no value for the form of rheumatism usually present in birds, but might be valuable in the case of sore swollen joints. The dose for birds is ¼ to ½ grain dissolved in an ounce of drinking water.

Sulphuric Acid. This is a mineral acid made from sulphur-dioxide, oxygen, and water, with the chemical formula H_2SO_4. It is a violent caustic poison and is not used in medicine except in very much diluted solutions.

Aromatic Sulphuric Acid, U. S. P.," is a preparation of sulphuric acid with alcoholic tincture of ginger and oil of cinnamon. It is a straw colored liquid with a peculiar aromatic odor and a pleasant acid taste when diluted, and is used both as an astringent and as a tonic. It is highly recommended as a tonic for birds in a rundown condition, especially for those suffering from liver trouble or from the effects of overfeeding. The dose is 1 to 2 drops to the ounce of drinking water in glass drinkers every other day.

Tartaric Acid. This is the acid found in grape juice. It is found on the market in the form of colorless crystals or a white powder, and has a strongly acid taste. The chemical formula is $(CH)_2(OH)_2(COOH)_2$. It is soluble in 1 part of water.

This acid is used as a physic, as a diuretic and in the preparation of effervescent mixtures. Inasmuch as the pure acid is very irritating to the stomach this substance is usually given greatly diluted in the form of grape juice or in combination with alkaline substances. Tartaric acid is an ingredient of Seidlitz powder, and of most of the other effervescent physics on the market. It cleans the bowels very quickly by causing large quanti-

---

[11]The letters U. S. P. are the initials of the United States Pharmacopoeia, which was adopted as the standard for the country in the Food & Drug Acts of June 30, 1906, and is issued every ten years after a revision by a national convention of physicians and pharmacists.

ties of water to be poured into them from the blood. It also causes a greatly increased flow of urine. This acid is of great value in the treatment of fevers and also rheumatic conditions in birds, but it is never used alone. It is one of the ingredients of Stroud's Specific. Its action on the bowels is much more intense than that of citric acid, but as a diuretic citric acid is preferable. One part of tartaric acid and one part of bicarbonate of soda can be mixed with several parts of many other salts, such as sodium phosphate, sodium sulphate, and others that do not dissolve easily in cold water, and the effervescent action adds greatly in the solution of the other salts.

This concludes the list of acid drugs that are of value in the treatment of bird's diseases. Most of these acids are not used in the pure state but only in dilutions and mixtures. Many of them form a long list of salts, some of which are of great value and will be discussed later. I may as well repeat here the warning that I have given several times in this section. Always give acid drugs, and for that matter all drugs, in glass drinkers. All acids dissolve metals and many other substances to form salts, some of which are extremely poisonous. Many cages nowadays are fitted with composition cups in fancy colors. Without knowing the composition from which such cups are made it would be impossible to tell which of these are safe and which are not; so it is best to be cautious and administer drugs in glass vessels only.

Aluminum and Potassium Sulphate. (Potassium Alum), U. S. P., is found commercially as a white powder or as large colorless crystals. Its chemical formula is $Al_2K_2(SO_4)_4$ plus $24H_2O$. It has an astringent taste and an acid reaction and is used to stop bleeding.

Ammoniac. This is a gum-resin from either a tree or some other kind of plant that has its habitat in

Northern India and Persia. It comes as round "tears" of irregular size, yellow outside and white inside. Ammoniac contains volatile oil, resin, salicylic acid, resinotannol, gum, and ferulic acid. It has a sweetish, bitter taste and is partly soluble in water, alcohol, and vinegar (dilute acetic acid). It is a diuretic and diaphoretic.

Preparation. Mix three parts of dilute acetic acid, containing 6% CH_3COOH, with one part of pure grain alcohol. To each ounce of this solution add 15 grains of powdered Ammoniac. Mix in a glass beaker and heat almost to the boiling point. While still hot pour into a bottle and stopper tightly. Shake at frequent intervals for several hours and then let stand over night. Filter through cotton and place in a tightly stoppered bottle.

This is used in the treatment of colds, chronic catarrh, and asthma. The dose for a bird is three to ten drops to the ounce drinker, which may be given daily for one week but should then be discontinued for several days before the treatment is repeated.

Ammonium Benzoate. This is one of the salts of benzoic acid. It comes on the market in the form of white crystals with a slightly benzoin odor and bitter salty taste. It is soluble in 5 parts of water and the chemical formula is $NH_4C_7H_5O_2$. It is an antiseptic, diuretic, antipyretic, and alterative. An alterative, it may be said, is a drug that has a beneficial effect upon the general health, the reason for which is not understood. It is a tonic without containing any of the known tonic elements.

Ammonium Benzoate is used in bronchitis, asthma, and gastro-intestinal disorders. Dose for a canary is $\frac{1}{8}$ to $\frac{1}{2}$ grain to the ounce of drinking water. The solution should be mixed daily and the drug should be kept in a tightly stoppered bottle and in a cool place. It loses ammonia when exposed to the air.

Bismuth, Bi. This is a hard and brittle, grayish-white metal with a reddish tinge which forms a long list of salts that are used in medicine, principally as antiseptics for dressing wounds and for internal use in diarrhoea, intestinal inflammation, and gastric ulcers. A few of the most important are the following:

Bismuth Citrate. This is a salt of bismuth and citric acid, which comes commercially as white microscopic crystals or a white amorphous powder, odorless and tasteless; its chemical formula is $BiC_6H_5O_7$. Citrate of Bismuth is a stomach stimulant and astringent.

The dose for a bird, 1/20 to 1/100 of a grain, may be prepared by grinding up one grain of the salt with 100 grains of sugar and then dusting it lightly on moist bread or egg-food. This salt is rather unstable and must be well stoppered and kept from the light. For that reason it is not often given to birds.

Bismuth Lactate. This is a salt of bismuth and lactic acid (the acid of milk) and is used as an intestinal antiseptic. It comes as a white powder or white crystals, whose chemical formula is $C_3H_5O_3 \cdot BiH_2H_4O_3$. This lactate is used in diarrhea prepared in the same manner as the citrate, except that the dose is five times as large; five grains of salt are mixed with 100 grains of sugar.

Bismuth Subgallate is the basic bismuth salt of gallic acid. It is found commercially as an odorless, saffron-yellow powder, insoluble in water. The chemical formula for this substance is $Bi(OH)_2C_7H_5O_5$, and it is prepared for use much as in the case of the other salts mentioned, except that four grains of the subgallate are used to 100 grains of sugar. I have found this one of the best salts of bismuth to use in cases of simple diarrhea in canaries.

It is very good too for weanlings that are raised in the flying hatch. Such weanlings will often eat things that are not good for them before they learn how to care for themselves well and may have a few days of diarrhea. This trouble, where the place is reasonably clean, is rarely fatal. Nevertheless it is best to treat it as a matter of prophylaxis, without, however, carrying the dosing to extremes.

With regard to this latter point, I know that many breeders reading the dosages here indicated will laugh and remark that they never took the trouble to dilute these drugs but sprinkled them on the soft food the way they came from the drug store. I need only to remind them that they might have saved their birds much trouble had they taken a little themselves. A bird is a very small creature. It is not so sensitive to some poisons as we are, and may take larger doses without fatal results, but that is no reason for giving it all or more than it can stand. The smallest dose of any medicine that will do the work required is always best.

Bismuth Subnitrate is a mixed salt of bismuth and nitric acid. Its chemical formula is $BiNO_3(OH)_2$ and $BiNO\ BiOOH$. The U. S. P. standard contains not less than 80% bismuth oxide, Bi_2O_3. This heavy white powder is the most used of all the bismuth salts. Many breeders feed it dusted on bread, but I think it should be diluted in the proportion of 15 parts of the salt to 85 parts of sugar.

The action of bismuth in the body. Most bismuth salts are decomposed in the stomach and intestine into the acid and the metallic oxide. This oxide of bismuth is a very heavy white powder, having the unique property of sticking to any sore or inflamed surface and forming a protective coating over the inflamed part. It is highly insoluble and for that reason can have no poisonous effect on the body. It also prevents the growth of bacteria. The subnitrate and the subgallate are used more frequently than the other compounds because they contain a very high percentage of bismuth and are less toxic than some of the other salts.

Bismuth is indicated only in case of simple diarrhoea. It is of no direct value in treating diarrhoea that is due to a general infection like septic fever or typhoid. It may help to relieve the painful symptoms but does nothing to cure the disease which is just as sure to prove fatal as if the bismuth had not been given. Such diseases must be treated by way of the blood.

Calcium, Ca, is a soft white metal that oxidizes quickly when exposed to the air. The free metal is little used, but it forms a large number of compounds that are of great importance. Quick lime is calcium oxide; water slaked lime is calcium hydroxide; limestone, egg-shell, marble, oyster-shell, pearls, cuttle-bone, and many other familiar substances are composed wholly or in part of calcium carbonate.

Besides being a necessary component of the blood and bones of animals and birds, and hence a constituent of any well balanced diet, there are a number of calcium salts that are of value for strictly medical purposes, of which I shall consider here only the most important.

Calcium Glycerinophosphate is made from calcium carbonate and glycerinophosphoric acid. Although soluble in thirty parts of water at room temperature, it is almost insoluble in boiling water. This salt is used as a nerve tonic and is of value in treating birds that are in a badly run-down condition from starvation, shipping about, sickness, or mistreatment. It can be given in the water 1/16 to ⅛ grain to the ounce every other day.

Calcium Permanganate is the calcium salt of permanganic acid. It comes in violet colored crystals that are easily soluble in water, forming a deep violet solution. The chemical formula is $Ca(MnO_4)_2$ plus $5H_2O$, and in general appearance this salt resembles the other permanganates. It has a less disagreeable taste than the corresponding potassium salt, and is no more poisonous to the body, but as an antiseptic it is more than 100 times as powerful as potassium permanganate. It is an even stronger antiseptic than mercury bichloride.

I have found no report of this substance ever being used in the treatment of bird fevers and have not had the chance to test it out for myself; but it seems reasonable that it might well replace potassium permanganate in the bird breeder's medicine cabinet, both for internal and external use. For fevers it could be used in 1 to 1000 or 1 to 2000 solution in water and still be a more powerful antiseptic than the potassium salt. For external use in the treatment of sores it could be used in 1% to 2% solution.

Calcium Peroxide comes as a yellow powder or in crystals, soluble in water with the evolution of oxygen. The chemical formula is CaO_2 plus $4H_2O$. It is recommended for use in acid dyspepsia and in summer diarrhea in infants. It is an antiacid and antiseptic as well as a source of oxygen.

This, like the drug just described, is one that has not, to my knowledge, ever been tested on birds, but one that holds great promise for the successful treatment of fevers if administered with alkaline solutions of citrates and phosphates. The dose for a canary would be about one grain to the ounce of drinking water or a 50% dilution with sugar dusted on bread. There is reason to believe that in the treatment of contagious fevers this suggested remedy would prove far superior to the use of either permanganates or chlorates and would be second only to my specific in effectiveness, though considerably more expensive.

Calcium Tribasic Phosphate is made from bone ash; its chemical formula is $Ca_3(PO_4)_2$. It is insoluble in water but soluble in acids, sometimes being used in bone diseases. This is the identical form in which phosphate is excreted by birds, the white end on the dropping of a healthy bird owing its color to this substance. It is merely as a matter of passing interest that it is mentioned here. When it is desired to give more phosphates than are present in the diet, they may be given to well birds in the form of sodium phosphate and bone meal in the mineral food and to run-down birds in the form of syrup of hypophosphites.

Calcium Saccharate is made from lime and sugar and comes in white glossy scales. It is easily soluble in sweetened water and is used in indigestion and for the removal of intestinal worms.

In treating the canary it should be diluted with three parts of sugar and fed on moist bread or other soft food. For indigestion the food is dusted lightly; for worms the amount given must be greater but not of course so large as to make the bird refuse the food. In the treatment of worms it should be followed by a cathartic of some kind.

Camphor Gum is derived from certain trees growing in subtropical Asiatic countries and is purchasable in the form of a white translucent mass that is easily broken up but is too gummy to reduce to a powder. It has a characteristic odor, is sometimes used in human medicine, but there appears to be no place for it in the treatment of birds.

Camphor, however, is much used as an insecticide in

DRUGS

the bird room. One ounce of camphor dissolved in one quart of turpentine and one quart of coal-oil may be used to paint the cracks of the cages. This treatment is very effective, but no more so than other methods that are both cheaper and easier to apply. Moth balls dissolved in turpentine and used the same way are effective for a much longer time than is camphor. Unpainted cages can be painted with disinfectant and thus mite-proofed for a whole year at a single treatment. Painted cages are best washed or sprayed with Fly-Tox.

Cascara Sagrada—U. S. P. This is the bark of a tree growing in the northwestern part of the United States from northern Idaho to northern California. The bark contains emodin, $C_{15}H_{10}O_5$; frangulin, $C_{21}H_{20}O_9$; three resins, tannin purshianin, cascarin; chrysarobin; chrysophanic acid; and fixed and volatile oils. It is used as a cathartic and tonic in the form of extracts, of which there are several.

The only preparation of cascara that is of value in treating birds is the Aromatic Fluid Extract of Cascara Sagrada. It contains cascara, licorice, magnesia, compound spirit of orange, and 25% of glycerin, and is a valuable constituent of a large number of tonic preparations for birds. The following are very useful:

(1) Aromatic cascara, one part; fluid extract of gentian, one part; licorice syrup, two parts; tincture of opium, one part; 50% ethyl alcohol, four parts. This is a very valuable paregoric tonic to use on birds recovering from serious diseases. If the paregoric properties of the opium are not needed, this can be omitted. The dose is from one to three drops to the ounce of drinking water. In the treatment of birds that have suffered a severe attack of the gastro-enteritic form of apoplectiform septicemia this prescription is of great value. It is also good

in the case of colds and of the early stages of pneumonia.

(2) The same preparation as (1) excepting that it contains one part of creosote. This is of more value in the treatment of severe bowel and lung infections because the creosote acts as an antiseptic in the lungs and bowels. It is of less value as a general tonic since creosote irritates the stomach.

Cascara can also be combined with sarsaparilla, quassia, and a number of other tonic extracts with good results.

Chrysanthemum Flowers. (Pyrethrum). This is a brownish-yellow powder that is made from the dried petals of these flowers which grow in Western Asia and in Asia Minor. Its constituents are: volatile oil; chrysanthemic acid; pyrethrotoxic acid; chrysthemin; and possibly a crystaline glucoside. There seems to be some doubt among chemists regarding the existence of this last mentioned constituent.

This article is a powerful insecticide and is largely used on birds to kill gray lice, which live and breed in the feathers. Because it is non-poisonous to birds, it is of considerable value for protecting the nest against lice and mites. It can be dusted on either the eggs or baby birds without harm if the dusting is not too heavy, but they should not be smothered with it.

A very little at a time is sufficient. I use outside nest boxes and always powder the nest well when I set the eggs, leaving at the same time considerable powder on the edges of the nest so that it will work down as the hen gets in and out. Thereafter I never shoot the powder directly into the nest, but instead I blow a good spray of it against the top of the nest box, allowing it to settle over the hen.

Cinchona, U. S. P., is the dried bark of the cinchona

or calisaya tree, which is native to Peru but is now cultivated in many other countries. The bark comes on the market in quills or flat sticks of various sizes; the external surface is gray and the internal surface an ochre yellow. It is also purchasable as a light cinnamon brown powder with a slight aromatic odor and a persistent bitter taste. Cinchona contains between 30 and 40 natural cinchona alkaloids (the chief of which is quinine); cinchotannic acid; quinic acid; volatile oils; and quinovic acid. It is an antiseptic, antipyretic, and astringent; and is used as a bitter tonic, as a treatment for fevers, especially malaria, as a treatment for coughs and colds, and as a source of quinine.

Cinchona is a valuable addition to bird tonics; it may also be used as a tonic by itself. For this purpose either the tincture or the compound tincture is used, and one to two drops to the ounce of drinking water is the correct dose. It should not be continued for more than one week at a time as overdosing with quinine often produces certain poisonous effects. Moreover, it is an odd feature of quinine poisoning that a subject once poisoned with it is thereafter highly susceptible to its poisonous action, and often very serious symptoms follow the administrations of even the most minute doses.

Copper Sulphate (Cupric sulphate; blue vitriol) large blue crystals that are easily soluble in water; the chemical formula is $CuSO_4$ plus $5H_2O$. Copper sulphate is used as a styptic (to stop bleeding), as an antiseptic, emetic, alterative, and nervine. All the cupric salts are very poisonous to bacteria and for that reason have been tested in a large number of diseases. They are poisonous to the higher animals, as well, and for that reason are not much used in medicine at the present time. This salt under discussion, however, is highly recommended for the treatment of septicemic diseases in birds. Given in the drinker, the dose recommended is five or six grains to the quart of water. I have not tested this substance myself but have reports from other breeders who say that very good results can be obtained by giving the copper sulphate solution for drinking water for half of each day and for the other half day giving orange juice in place of water for the birds to drink.

Creolin. (Sometimes called compound cresols, and also known by such trade names as Phenoline, carboleneum, and a host of others.) It is composed of the crude mixed creosotes of coal tar saponified with sodium hydroxide. Creolin is a powerful germicide, antiseptic, deodorant, and considerably more powerful as a disinfectant than carbolic acid. It is sold as a dark brown or black syrupy liquid that forms a milky emulsion with water.

Creolin is used by the bird breeder in ½ to 1% solution to wash cages, as an antiseptic for the hands and as an insecticide. For the latter purpose it can be used in solution as a wash or spray mixed with either oil or water, or it may be used in full strength to paint woodwork in the bird room. Woodwork so painted once or twice each year will not harbor mites.

Creosote is purchasable as a colorless or faintly yellow liquid with a characteristic smoky odor and a burning taste. It is caustic, antiseptic, anthelmintic (kills worms), and antipyretic. Of the numerous kinds and grades of creosote, the only one which is used internally is made by distillation from the tar of beechwood. This grade of creosote is only slightly poisonous, while that obtained from coal-tar is highly poisonous. The chemical formula of creosote is $C_6H_3OCH_3 \cdot CH_3OH$. The creosote on the market, even the purest is really a mixture

DRUGS

of phenols and phenol-derivatives. Creosote is the largest constituent with guaiacol, $C_5H_4(OCH_3)OH$ next in size. Creosote is soluble in all proportions with alcohol, ether, chloroform, and acetic acid, but is only slightly soluble in water.

I have mentioned the use of creosote as a tonic and intestinal antiseptic in the discussion of prescriptions containing cascara. If creosote is given in large doses, about ten drops to the ounce of drinking water, it becomes a valuable treatment for worms. There is also a standard prescription on the market known as Waterberry's Tonic with Creosote. This is used in tuberculosis of the lungs in human beings and also in digestive troubles. Given from 5 to 7 drops to the ounce of drinking water it is an excellent treatment for intestinal worms in canaries. It should be given for two or three days or until the bird starts to show some distress, then discontinued and sodium sulphate or phosphate given for a single day. This neutralizes the effects of the creosote on the system and at the same time acts on the bird as a cathartic, removing the dead and sluggish worms from the intestinal tract.

Gentian is the dried rhizome and roots of the plant *Gentiana lutea* which grows in Central and Southern Europe. It contains gentianin, $C_{14}H_{10}O_5$; gentiopicrin, $C_{20}H_{30}O_{12}$; gentianose; and pectin. A bitter tonic and laxative, it appears on the market as a dry powder, an aqueous extract, a fluid extract, an alcoholic tincture, and a compound tincture.

Gentian is a very valuable tonic for birds. It is indicated in all cases where the bird is run-down and has a poor appetite. One to three drops of the tincture or compound tincture can be given in the drinking water, or it may be compounded with buckthorn, cascara, licorice, honey, and other substances. The best prescription that I know of is the one given under the heading "Cascara".

Geranium is a plant native to the United States and Canada. There is a drug prepared from the dried rhizome of the plant, but it is of no particular interest to canary breeders. The red flowers of this plant are eaten by canaries with great relish, and, if fed fresh during the moulting season, they aid in giving the feathers that deep orange color that is so often sought. There are a great many red, yellow, and brown flowers, the fresh petals of which are of value in this respect, while at the same time acting as tonics to the birds and helping them over the moult. This is a much better system of color-feeding than the usual diet of red pepper, the drawback being that only the breeder with a garden at his disposal can take advantage of it.

Glycerin is an organic base obtained from the decomposition of fats. It comes as a thick, syrupy, colorless liquid that has a sweet, warm taste. The chemical formula is $C_3H_5(OH)_3$. Glycerine is soluble in all proportions in water and alcohol, having a great affinity for the former. It is sometimes used as a laxative, but its principal uses are in the dilution of drugs and in the preparation of ointments. It has the power of preventing other drugs that normally would be very irritating from doing harm; for example, tincture of iodine cannot be used upon a moist or mucous surface without harm, but mixed with equal parts of glycerin it can be used with safety. It is also of value in making ointments for treating scaly-leg. Carbolated vaseline is used for this but it is dangerous in that it may blister the bird. Mixing in a little glycerin will overcome this danger.

In septic fever and other infections the bird often breathes through its mouth for days at a time, causing the tongue to become dry and hard and making it impossible for the bird to eat. A drop of glycerin and olive oil mixed in equal parts placed in the beak several times every day while the bird is in this condition is of great value and may save it much suffering. Glycerin and honey may also be used. Usually in such cases the bird is very weak and the heart is in bad condition. One part of pure grain alcohol added to the honey and glycerin will be of value. This may be put into the beak or from 20 drops to a half teaspoonful of it may be mixed with an ounce of drinking water if other medicines are not being given in the water. If the diseases mentioned are being treated as they should be, however, there will be other substances in the drinking water that prevent this use of this mixture. Glycerine is also a good stimulant for birds with a bad cold.

Glycyrrhiza (Licorice). This is the dried root of a Spanish plant by the name of *Glycyrrhiza glabra*. It has only moderate laxative and stimulating properties but is principally used to disguise the taste of unpleasant drugs. For this purpose, the fluid extract of this substance or the extract mixed with honey or syrup is used.

Glycyrrhizin Ammoniate. The natural sweetening substance from licorice is also used to disguise the flavor of unpleasant drugs and is itself a remedy for coughs and colds.

Glycerite, Iron, Quinine, and Strychnine Phosphates —U.S.P. This is a solution of soluble ferric phosphate (80 parts), quinine (104), strychnine (0.8), phosphoric acid (200), glycerin (500), and water to make up a thousand parts. Dose for a bird is one drop to the ounce of water.

Hexamethylenamine (Urotropin). This is a complex chemical product having the formula $(CH_2)_6 N_4$. Urotropin is found on the market in the form of white crystals or powder, is soluble in water and to a slight extent in alcohol. This drug is one of the most valuable that modern chemistry has added to human medicine. It is an antiseptic and diuretic, one of the few internal antiseptics known that are effective.

Hexamethylenamine is principally used in infections of the kidneys and in rheumatic conditions, but it is of great value in a wide range of infectious diseases in human beings. It acts only when the solution in which it is contained has an acid reaction. When the blood, and especially the urine of the infected subject, is acid, this substance undergoes chemical decomposition with the liberation of formaldehyde. Inasmuch as the chemical is excreted in the urine and since the reaction of the urine can easily be made acid by the administration of sodium acid phosphate or sodium benzoate, it follows that it is of considerable value in kidney infections, or in general disease in which the kidneys are involved.

Unfortunately I have not yet had the opportunity to test this drug upon canaries, but there is every reason to believe that it would prove of great value in the treatment of septicemic diseases. It is my plan to test it thoroughly upon the next group of experimental birds that I obtain. I offer the following suggestion in the hope that perhaps others will also test it.

This drug can usually be had in three grain and five grain tablets at any drug store. Five grains of hexamethylenamine should be ground with 95 grains of sugar and about one grain of this dusted on some soft food of which the bird is fond. At the same time one grain of acid sodium phosphate should be added to the ounce of drinking water.

Hydrogen Peroxide is an oily explosive liquid ob-

DRUGS 201

tained from the action of powerful oxidizing agents upon water. Because it is very unstable in the pure state, it is put up in 3% and 30% water solutions. The three percent solution is the one usually sold in drug stores under the name of "Peroxide of Hydrogen." This is known as the "ten volume solution," for each volume gives off ten times its own bulk in oxygen gas. Peroxide of Hydrogen is a very powerful antiseptic. The 3% solution has a germ killing power equal to 1:1000 solution of mercury bichloride.

Peroxide of Hydrogen has the power to counteract the poisonous effects of cyanide, abrin, diptheria, and tetanus toxins. It is of great value in treating the contagious bird diseases. The discovery of this led to making it the basis of my specific for avian septicemias. Any breeder with any of these diseases in his flock will do well to read carefully my directions for the use of Peroxide of Hydrogen in their treatment; as it is second only to my specific in its value, and the very same principle and reaction is employed. It is second to my specific because the reaction that kills the germs in the blood is more difficult to control, the amount of available oxygen is less, and the cost of a prolonged treatment is much greater.

Iodine is a chemical element that was formerly extracted from the ash of sea-weed. It is now obtained as a by-product of the Chile nitrate industry. The pure element is put on the market in the form of bluish-black plates, having a metallic luster, a peculiar odor, and a sharp, acrid taste. Iodine itself is not used in medicine but many of its salts and solutions which are the substances actually employed are of great value. Iodine is a powerful antiseptic and fungicide. It is a necessity in processes of the thyroid gland, but for this the free element is not used as it cannot be assimilated. On the contrary this acts as a poison when taken into the body.

Tincture of Iodine is an alcoholic solution containing 7% iodine and 5% potassium iodide. It is largely used to sterilize the skin for operations; to treat local skin infections, especially those due to pathogenic moulds such as actinomycosis and ring-worm; to treat such acute infections as diphtheria and erysipelas; to sterilize wounds and reduce swellings. A cotton swab or soft brush are convenient means for applying this remedy. If applied to wet skin or mucous membrane, or if applied too thickly to the dry skin, it may blister or even destroy the skin. To avoid this destructive action the tincture is often mixed with from one to three parts of glycerin.

Iron is a grayish-white metal with which everyone is familiar. While iron itself is not used either in food or in medicine, very many of the compounds of iron are of great importance in both. This element was mentioned earlier in the discussion of feeding. In the following paragraphs only a few of the iron preparations that are of value will be discussed.

Iron Acetate is the ferric salt of acetic acid. The chemical formula is $Fe_2(C_2H_3O_2)_6$. This acetate appears on the market in the form of brownish red scales and is used as a tonic. It is also put up for the same purpose in a 31% solution. The dose for a canary would be 1/5 drop to the ounce of drinking water, or one drop to five ounces of drinking water.

Iron Chloride, U.S.P. This is purchasable in orange-yellow crystals that are very deliquescent (absorb water out of the air to dissolve themselves). They have an astringent taste, and are soluble in water and alcohol. The formula for this substance is $FeCl_3$ plus $6H_2O$. Iron chloride is used externally to stop bleeding and internally as a tonic. This salt is the basis of the solution known as "tincture of iron."

Tincture of iron is made by mixing 350 parts of a hydro-alcoholic solution of iron chloride containing 13.28% of $FeCl_3$ with 650 parts of alcohol. It is a bright brown liquid, having a slight ethereal odor and a very astringent taste. Used as a tonic, the dose for a canary is one drop to three ounces of water.

Iron Citrate, the ferric salt of citric acid, is found on the market in the form of reddish brown scales. Its chemical formula is approximately $Fe_2(C_6H_5O_7)_2$ plus $6H_2O$. When this citrate is used as a tonic, the best form of it for use on birds is the Effervescent Citrate of Iron.

Effervescent Citrate of Iron, containing citrate of iron, tartaric acid, and carbonate of soda, is a standard preparation and can be bought put up ready to use. It is sensitive to light and hence must be kept in the dark. The dose for a canary is ¼ grain to the ounce of drinking water. It is useful in soft moult but not so useful as some of the compound citrates that will be mentioned later.

Syrup of Iron Citro-Iodine, a syrupy solution containing 6% iron iodide and 8.5% of potassium citrate, is a valuable tonic for birds that are in a run-down condition from disease or from too much breeding. The dose, one drop to two or three ounces of drinking water, should be given not longer than one week at a time if given continuously, but if given every other day the treatment may be continued for several weeks.

Iron Ammonium Citrate is purchasable in the form of reddish-brown scales and is used like other mild iron tonics. It has been highly recommended as a cure for soft moult, the dose for a canary being ⅛ grain to the ounce of drinking water.

Iron Sulphate, the ferrous salt of iron and sulphuric

acid, appears commercially in the form of large blue-green crystals (formula $FeSO_4$ plus $7H_2O$) and is commonly called cuprous or green vitriol. This substance is a very powerful antiseptic and is highly recommended for the treatment of septic fever, canary necrosis, and B Paratyphosus B infection in birds. The dose is 5 or 6 grains to the quart of drinking water.

Elixir of Iron, Quinine, and Strychnine Phosphates is a yellowish-green tonic with a pleasant citric taste when diluted. It contains in every 1000 parts the following:

Soluble Ferric Phosphate	17.500	parts or grams
Quinine	8.750	" " "
Strychnine	00.275	" " "
Phosphoric Acid	2.000	" " "
Ammonium carbonate, translucent pieces	9.000	" " "
Alcohol	60.000	" " "
Acetic Acid	28.650	" " "

Ammonia water, distilled water, and Aromatic Elixir to make up 1000 parts or cubic centimeters as the unit of measure may be.

Note: The Aromatic Elixir is made from

Compound Spirits of Orange	12 cc
Syrup	375 cc
Purified talc	30 cc

Alcohol and distilled water to make up 1000 cc.

This is used in the preparation of many prescriptions, since the spirits of orange and the syrup kill the taste of bitter drugs.

The Elixir of I.Q.S. is the justly famous iron, quinine, and strychnine tonic which I have mentioned so often in my discussion of the treatment of birds that are out of condition. The dose for a bird is one to two drops in the

DRUGS

ounce of drinking water. Three or even four drops may be given for a single day as a stimulant (that is, to the ounce of drinking water—a dose that size put into the beak will cause death), but such doses must not be given very often. Two drops to the ounce of drinking water continued for from ten days to three weeks will cause convulsions due to strychnine poisoning. After the tonic is given for one week it is best to discontinue it for at least a week before giving it again to the bird. This tonic and the ones to be described in the next paragraph are the best medicines known for causing the feathers on a bird to tighten in soft moult, but of course no drug can do this if the conditions causing the soft moult are not attended to at the same time.

Iron and Quinine Citrate—Brown— is obtainable in the form of reddish brown, deliquescent scales that have a bitter ferruginous (characteristic of iron) taste. It contains 11.5% of quinine and 13.5% of iron, and is used as a tonic; it is not, however, so useful as the green variety.

Iron and Quinine Citrate—Green—appears in the form of greenish-yellow, transparent, deliquescent scales having the bitter characteristic iron taste. This substance is a tonic, astringent, and antipyretic. In addition to the quinine ferrocitrate it contains ammonia, is much more soluble than the brown variety, and contains the same percentages of iron and quinine. The dose for a bird is about $\frac{1}{8}$ grain to the ounce of drinking water. This preparation is used as a tonic and in treating soft moult. While less valuable than I.Q.S. in acute diseases, it has in soft moult the advantage that its continued use will not cause convulsions. Many breeders use this salt as a panacea, some even going so far as to give all their birds a course of it before considering them to be in condition for the breeding season.

I. and Q. Citrate, put up in an effervescent form, is also of value. The formula is green I. and Q. Citrate, 2 parts; sodium bicarbonate, 60 parts; tartaric acid, 54 parts; sugar, 64 parts. This is a fine tonic laxative for feverish birds and it is also good for putting sluggish birds into breeding condition. The dose is 1 to 2 grains to the ounce of drinking water.

Iron, Quinine, and Strychnine Citrate is the same substance as the above excepting that it contains 1% of strychnine, thus requiring considerable diluting before it can be used on birds. It may be diluted by grinding one part of the salt with 24 parts of sugar, in which case each half grain of the resulting powder will contain approximately the same amount of strychnine as one drop of IQS. It may also be made the basis of a tonic as follows:

IQS Citrate 25	grams	or parts
Citric Acid 2	" "	"
Ammonium Carbonate 9	" "	"
Acetic Acid 28.6	" "	"
Alcohol 60	" "	"

Ammonia water, distilled water, and aromatic elixir to make up 1000 cc or parts.

Dissolve the citrate in the alcohol diluted with 60 parts of distilled water and add the citric acid and 300 parts of the aromatic elixir to the solution. Add the acetic acid to the ammonium carbonate and dissolve them in distilled water, using just enough to make a saturated solution. Then neutralize them with ammonia water. Mix the two solutions together and add enough aromatic elixir to constitute 1000 parts.

This mixture contains the same amount of strychnine

to each drop as does the I.Q.S. Phosphate tonic and is used in the same manner.

Note: All of these organic iron preparations should be kept in brown bottles, away from the light, and should be tightly stoppered. Otherwise they are apt to undergo chemical changes that may render them at best useless and perhaps harmful. Never use any of these preparations that has been exposed to the light and has changed in color.

Lime, Calcium Oxide, CaO, which is made by burning limestone or marble until the carbon-dioxide is driven off, is used to make white-wash for bird rooms and cages.

A good white-wash is made by slaking five pounds of lime in enough water to make a fluid of the consistency of syrup. Make a batter of one pound of flour. In another vessel let ½ pound of glue stand in cold water until softened; then add the glue to the batter and to this mixture add two quarts of water. Boil for half an hour, stirring enough to keep it from burning, and adding water if need be, to keep it the consistency of paste. Mix the hot paste with the slaked lime that has been permitted to cool from the heat of the reaction of slaking. To each five gallons of the wash add one teacupful of cresol. Thin with hot water as desired and apply. If the birds have not had plenty of lime in a more appetizing form before them, the cresol is best left out, for there is some danger of the birds eating the white-wash and thereby getting poisoned. In any case the room or the equipment white-washed should not be used until it is thoroughly dry. A charcoal burner placed in the room will assist in the drying by providing carbon-dioxide, which combines with the lime in the drying process, thus forming a hard white coating.

Lysol is a mixture of alkali compounds of the higher phenols with fat and resin soaps, which are obtained by boiling a mixture of heavy tar oils with fat, resin, and lye. Lysol is a brown or black fluid containing about 50% cresols. This general description fits the majority of the coal-tar disinfectants on the market, but they differ greatly in strength and germ-killing power. In using any of these commercial products it is advisable to note the carbolic coefficient, which tells you the germ-killing power of the product with reference to carbolic acid. This coefficient may vary from 2 to 20, the best grades having 10 times the germ-killing power of the poorest grades. A product having a coefficient of 5 should be used in the proportion of ½ ounce to the gallon to kill lice and mites, one ounce to the gallon to kill germs.

Most of these products are sold under trade names, but there is one purified product for which the makers claim the name "Lysol" as theirs exclusively. It is water-white and a very powerful disinfectant and antiseptic. This is the product that most persons have in mind when they use the name "Lysol", the others being usually referred to as "coal-tar disinfectants".

Naphthalene is a hydrocarbon from coal-tar with the chemical formula $C_{10}H_8$. Most of the moth balls on the market are now made from this powerful insecticide. White in the pure varieties, yellow or brown in the crude, it is an antiseptic, antidiarrhoea, anthelmintic, and antipyretic.

This substance has a wide range of uses in the bird room. It is very valuable in the storing of seeds. A handful of the balls scattered through a bag of seed will keep it free from worms and also tend to preserve it in a fresh state. My own system of storing seed is as follows:

I have a steel chest made from an old kitchen table by nailing a shelf to the legs five inches from the floor and then encasing it with sheet steel, providing a steel door in the front. Sacks, bags, and boxes of seed are placed in this cabinet and several handsful of naphthalene moth balls are scattered around inside. The amount of naphthalene absorbed by the seed will not be harmful to the birds.

Naphthalene may also be used to advantage in delousing nests as mentioned earlier in this book; and it has also been recommended for use in the nest while the bird is sitting. Tests made by me along this line show that it will kill some chicks in the egg, will kill eight-day old chicks in sixteen but not in twelve hours, will make the hen stupid but will not kill her as a rule. These results were obtained from placing moth balls in the nest and from strongly impregnating the nest material with naphthalene. A small pinch of the powdered substance placed between the nest and the lining is, however, without harm to the birds and will do wonders in keeping the nest free from lice and mites.

This substance is used in acute and chronic inflammation of the intestines, catarrh, worms, typhoid, cholera, and chronic bronchitis in human subjects. I have not tested its reaction on birds suffering with acute contagious diseases, but it will lower the temperature, relieve diarrhoea, cure some colds and throat ailments, and remove worms from the intestines.

For diarrhoea and colds it may be diluted with sugar in the proportion of 1:100 and the dose is from $\frac{1}{2}$ to 1 grain on soft food; for worms it is diluted 1:20 and the dose is $\frac{1}{2}$ to 1 grain on soft food.

Warning: Overdoses of this substance are likely to cause death but only when the bird is neglected. At the first symptom of naphthalene poisoning the bird becomes dopy, and if the treatment is discontinued at once the patient will usually recover without further aid. Even if the bird is so far gone that it is down at the bottom of the cage in coma, it can as a rule be saved by putting it in a very warm place and feeding it I.Q.S. two drops to the ounce of warm water. The solution is put into the beak, a drop or two at a time, until the bird recovers sufficiently to move around.

Naphthalene is sometimes fed to poultry to make their feathers lice-proof. I have tried this remedy on birds but do not approve of its use for canaries. Where a large number of birds are kept in flight and it is impractical to powder them for lice, fair results can be had by removing the bath for a day and giving them drinking water in receptacles in which it is impossible for them to bathe. Then dissolve three moth balls in eight ounces of alcohol (get a prescription for this and make sure that grain alcohol is used), and when the bath is returned (which should be about mid-day) one teaspoonful of the alcoholic solution of naphthalene should be added to each quart of bath water. This will effectively delouse any birds that bathe in it and without harm to them; but due to the smell of the water only a few of them will use this bath. Quassia infusion is much recommended for this purpose, but comparative tests made with quassia and naphthalene, used as just described, showed the naphthalene to be much more effective than the quassia, from which no good results could be noted. Tests were compared by catching all of the birds once each week, removing all of the lice eaten feathers, and counting the number of feathers removed as an index to the extent of the louse infection. The results were:

Quassia—No reduction in extent of infection when used daily for three weeks. Doubtless because the solution made from the Quassia was obtained by boiling, which, I have been told, reduces its efficiency to zero. When made by allowing the quassia to stand in cold water it is said to be efficacious, but I cannot report on this personally.

Naphthalene—30% reduction the first week, 50% reduction the second week, 65% reduction in three weeks. No reduction beyond that. The birds using the bath were entirely freed from lice but the infection on those that refused to use the bath was greatly increased.

Note: Where naphthalene is intended for internal use only, the pure white medical variety should be used. The crude brown moth balls are all right for storing seed or delousing nests.

Nasturtium is an herb from plants of the nasturtium family, of which watercress and the common garden flowers are two most important members. This herb is credited with being of value in treating fevers, neuralgia, etc. Of the value of the dried herb in the treatment of bird diseases I know little, but the leaves of the fresh plants are one of the best forms of green food for birds; and the flowers, especially of the red variety, are of great value as a color producing food. The breeder who can give his birds a large bouquet of these red flowers every day will not have to worry about some of his birds not eating the pepper food. The color is not so rich as that produced by pepper, but it falls little short in that respect; and it is much easier to produce nice evenly colored birds by feeding these and other flowers than by feeding pepper.

Nux Vomica is the dried ripe seed of the plant *Strychnos Nux Vomica, L. Loganiaceae.* It contains strychnine, brucine, loganin, igasuric acid, and proteids. Used as a stimulant and tonic in human medicine, it has the power to settle the stomach and to stop vomiting; hence its name. Many breeders recommend Nux Vomica as a stimulant and tonic for birds, but I prefer to use strychnine in the form of I. Q. S.

Nux Vomica is found on the market in several preparations of which the dried alcohol extract is the strongest. The fluid extract is about $\frac{1}{4}$ as strong; the dried aqueous extract about the same strength as the fluid extract; and the tincture is only $\frac{1}{5}$ as strong as the fluid extract. The dose, usually given in cooked oatmeal, is five drops to the quart. It may be used in water in this strength but should be discontinued should the birds develop nervousness or convulsions.

Castor Oil is obtained by pressing the seed of *Ricinus Communis,* the castor oil bean. This is often recommended as a cathartic for birds, but my experience hae been that it is a product that could be dropped profitably from both human and bird medicine. The dose recommended for a canary is one or two drops—I have never seen a bird survive a dose that size and have seen no effects due to its use which cannot be brought about by other methods that are less harmful. I am not very much in favor of the internal use of oils as cathartics for birds, but if it seems absolutely necessary to use an oil, olive oil will be found quite strong enough as a cathartic and at the same time harmless.

Cod Liver Oil is a pale yellow oil rendered from the livers of codfish. It contains in addition to the animal fat organic iodides, free fatty acids, and biliary products. It should also be rich in vitamins A and D. I have discussed the use of this oil under the heading of feeding. The dose for a canary is from 3 to 10 drops in the egg-food made from one egg. The best grade of this oil I have found, Squibb's Pure Cod Liver Oil, is treated with carbonic acid in such a way as to kill the putrid taste and preserve the vitamines. The birds like it; they eat the food containing it without difficulty.

Olive Oil. This pale yellow oil pressed from ripe olives is a mild laxative and also a nutrient. The best grades usually contain some vitamin A and D in addition to their fats. As a laxative three drops put into the beak is the correct dosage for a canary.

Orange Oil is a light yellow oil pressed from the fresh rinds of *Citrus Vulgaris* and other citrus fruits. It is of value in flavoring bird foods.

Opium is the dried milk of the unripe poppy, and contains a large number of narcotic alkaloids, the chief of which are morphine and cotine. Opium itself is not used in bird medicine, but tincture of opium, which is the 10% solution of opium in alcohol, is used in practically all paregoric mixtures. One prescription using this substance was given earlier under the heading "Cascara." Standard paregoric is a 1:250 solution of opium and contains 0.12 grams of opium to each 30 grams, together with camphor, benzoic acid, oil of anise, and glycerin. The right dose for a canary is 3 to 5 drops to the ounce of drinking water.

Blue Maw Seed is the seed of the opium poppy and the hulls contain a very small amount of this drug. In most cases where opium is indicated for birds it can be given by feeding this seed. All birds are very fond of the seed and they do not get enough of the drug in this manner to be harmed. There is the further consideration that prescriptions containing opium can only be filled with some difficulty and red tape, while maw seed is, or should be, present in every bird room.

Potassium Chlorate is the potassium salt of chloric acid; its chemical formula is $KClO_3$. It comes on the market in the form of colorless crystals or as a white powder, having a cool, salty taste. This is a powerful oxidizing antiseptic which has been used successfully in septic fever. While poisonous, it is less so than potassium permanganate.

Of seven birds treated in one of my experiments designated as experiment No. 1 four died; three recovered within from three to seven days after commencing treatment. The birds had the pox form of the disease. They were given ¼ grain of potassium chlorate to the ounce of drinking water for the first half day of each day. For the second half of each day they were given my effervescent salt mixture in their drinking water. Sores were treated with potassium permanganate.

In experiment No. 2 twelve birds suffering with the pneumonic form of the disease were treated for 35 days, and in that time two of them died. None of the others recovered under the treatment, but eight recovered under treatment with my specific. The two that died had developed sores and died of heart failure while the sores were being treated. In this case the treatment was given in the proportion of 3 to 7 drops of saturated solution of the chlorate to each ounce of drinking water along with one grain of Sal-Hepatica. These results are notable, not because they offer means of curing and controlling this disease, but because they do provide a method of preventing deaths from the disease during the time it may take to secure more effective treatment.

Caution: Potassium chlorate should never be mixed

with powdered combustibles as it forms explosive mixtures with such matter.

Potassium Iodide is the potassium salt of hydro-iodic acid; its chemical formula is KI. It comes on the market in the form of colorless crystals or as a white granular powder, soluble in about 0.75 parts of water at room temperature. The solution contains about 100 drops to the dram, each drop containing about one half grain of the salt. It is best used in a saturated solution since by this method the dosage can be measured very accurately. Large doses of this substance are poisonous. Antidote: sodium bicarbonate solution, one teaspoonful to the glass of water.

Potassium Iodide is a very important salt. It is an alterative, a uric acid solvent, a fungicide, and a source of assimilable iodine. This very powerful drug is needed by the system but in very small quantities, and should not be administered with acid, metal, or alkaloidal salts. For a general constitutional effect on birds that are raised at a distance from the sea, it is best given in the mineral food as described elsewhere. As an alterative, in rheumatism, liver trouble, colds, asthmatic breathing, and fungus infection, especially of the mucous membrane, it is given in the drinking water, one to three drops to the ounce of water. This drug is largely excreted through the skin and mucous membrane. When a saturated solution is taken by a human being in progressive doses (the dose for a human being should begin at 5 drops three times per day and increase at the rate of one drop per day until the system is saturated), there is at first no noticeable effect; but after a few days the taste becomes at first disagreeable and later sickening and persistent, so that toward the end of the treatment it can be tasted constantly while at the same time the nose and eyes water and the skin breaks out in pimples. This stimulated secretion from the mucous membrane, surcharged with the salt, provides one of the best methods we have of reaching certain infections of the mucous surfaces. This is especially true of thrush and aspergillus infection of the internal mucous surfaces. I have found this treatment one of the best that I have tried for chronic colds of an asthmatic nature. In my own room this treatment has practically displaced all others in the handling of this class of infection. It is not a treatment which brings rapid results and must be given constantly for at least one week before the system becomes saturated enough with the drug to bring about this prophylactic action; but a cure effected by its use is usually complete and leaves the subject in very much improved general health. A canary should never be given more than three drops to the ounce of drinking water, and if he then shows much distress, the treatment should be stopped for a day and Stroud's Effervescent Salts given.

Potassium Permanganate is the potassium salt of permanganic acid, sold in dark purple, slender, opaque, prismatic crystals, having a blue metallic reflection and a sweet, astringent taste. It is soluble in 16 parts of water at room temperature, is a powerful oxidizing antiseptic, and has been largely used in the treatment of bird fevers. I have found it of little value for internal treatment, but it is very effective for treating the sores. For direct application to the scarified sores it is used in saturated solution; for injection into the sores a two per cent solution is strong enough; for internal use it is given in a 1:500 or 1:1000 solution as drinking water. It is an antidote for morphine poisoning and snake bite, but in my opinion this salt could be advantageously displaced by the calcium salt.

DRUGS

Quassia is the wood and bark of the Bitterwood Trees, *Picrasma excelsa,* and *Quassia amara,* two distinct trees of closely related species which inhabit the West Indies. The first contains only two bitter principles; the latter, or true Quassia, contains four. The constituents are: Picrasmin, $C_{35}H_{46}O_{10}$; quassin, $C_{10}H_{12}O_3$ (?) (there is some doubt about the exact formula of this substance); quassol, $C_{40}H_7$ plus H_2O; alkaloid; resin; and pectin. It is used in the treatment of digestive disorders as a bitter tonic, in constipation, for internal worms, and for fevers. It is also used in the manufacture of fly poison and by bird breeders to kill mites. For this purpose one teaspoonful of aqueous infusion, made from steeping the chips overnight in hot water, is added to each five ounce bird bath."

Quassia comes in chips of the wood, of the bark, in alcohol extract, fluid extract, and tincture. I have not tested the tonic qualities of this substance on birds, but the dose would be 2 to 6 drops of the tincture to the ounce of drinking water. The fluid extract is three times as strong as the tincture, so that the maximum dose would be 2 drops to the ounce of drinking water.

Quinine is the principal alkaloid obtained from cinchona bark. Although the pure alkaloid is not much used, the substance forms a large number of salts that are very important as antipyretics, antiperiodics, antiseptics, and tonics. The sulphate (formula $(C_{20}H_{24}N_2O_2)_2 H_2SO_4 \cdot 7H_2O$) is one of the most important salts known to human medicine—one of the very few specifics known. Various combinations of this salt with opium and cathartic have provided us with the most effective treatments known for

---

[12] "I have been told by several druggists that steeping or boiling destroys the effectiveness of this, and have had good effects by using a solution of cold water in which the chips are left standing.— (Editor's Note.)

fevers of all kinds up until recently. This being the case, it is natural to suppose that the salt should be of value in treating bird diseases. My experiments with it in the treatment of septic fever were negative. This may have been due to the difficulties encountered in getting the salt into the bird in therapeutic quantities. The citrate, $(C_{20}H_{24}N_2O_2)_2C_6H_8O_7$ plus $7H_2O$, and the phosphate, $(C_{20}H_{24}N_2O_2)_2H_3PO_4$ plus $8H_2O$, are very valuable as tonics, and their use and preparation have been spoken of in connection with a discussion of the iron salts with which they are used in combination.

Silver Nitrate is the silver salt of nitric acid, $AgNO_3$. It is put on the market in the form of colorless rhombic plates, has a bitter taste and is very caustic. It is used in solutions of form 0.1% to 2% as an antiseptic, and is put up in sticks for use as a caustic in the **treatment of** growths and ingrown feathers. The latter, a disease of crested birds caused by double buffing and double cresting, is characterized by the formation of lumpy abscesses during the moult, and for that reason is known as "lumps." If the lump is opened, the feathers removed, and the spot washed out, it will heal and the bird will be all right until the next moult when the lump will return. An English veterinarian, Professor Tom Hare of the Royal Veterinary College, London, who has recently made a study of this disease, has discovered, however, that if the lump is burned out with silver nitrate it does not return at the next moult.[13]

Silver Protein Preparations: *Argenol,* 10% silver with albumoid; *Argentose,* 30% silver with nucleo-proteid; *Argyrol,* 20 to 25% silver with Vitellin.

There is a large number of these preparations, all

---

[13]His findings are reported in Cage Birds, London, October 31, 1931. I am indebted to J. Tomlinson, Stafford, England, for my information regarding this disease.

powerful antiseptics, of which argyrol is the most used. It is put up in from 10 to 25% solutions. I have found the 10% solution a wonderful remedy for irrigating the nose and throat in colds and similar infections. An eye dropper is held in an alcohol flame until the point is soft. The point is then stuck to another piece of glass and drawn out to a rather fine point, and then broken off where it will give a narrow end that just fits into a bird's nostril with ease. This end is again held in the flame to remove the rough edges. The instrument is then loaded with argyrol solution, the point placed in the nostril and enough of the solution injected so that some of it will come through into the bird's mouth. The same procedure is followed in the case of the other nostril, care being taken not to stain the feathers more than necessary. It is fortunate, however, that argyrol stains wash out in a few days if the bird bathes every day.

In using argyrol in the manner just described some of it is undoubtedly swallowed. The breeder should take care not to force the bird to swallow more than necessary; and the bird is perfectly willing to co-operate in this, for he does not like it and will spit out all that he can. He should be released from the hand as quickly as possible after applying the treatment so that he will have a chance to reject what is in the mouth. There are grounds for believing that too much of it would be harmful, but I have used the treatment every day for two weeks without noticing any deleterious effects on the bird.

Sodium is a silver-white metal, known by the chemical symbol Na. The pure metal is highly active and is not used in the bird room. Its only uses are technical. It combines spontaneously with both air and moisture so that it can be kept only when immersed in a liquid free from oxygen, such as coal oil or naphtha. This metal forms a large number of salts that are of great importance to the bird keeper.

Sodium Hydroxide. When metallic sodium is placed in contact with water or moisture it decomposes it with the consequent evolution of hydrogen and a great evolution of heat. The result is sodium hydroxide. Most of the sodium hydroxide on the market is made by blowing steam through a molten alloy of sodium and lead that is obtained by the electrical decomposition of common salt, the molten lead being used as the electrode at which the sodium collects. The resultant product of the action of steam on the sodium-lead alloy has an average composition of sodium hydroxide, 94%; sodium carbonate, 2%; sodium chloride, sodium sulphate, and moisture combined, about 4%. This is the history and approximate composition of the contents of ordinary lye that should be familiar in every bird room.

Lye is one of the best cleansing agents known for the reason that it has the power to form soluble soaps with all organic oils and other soluble compositions with most other organic compounds, as well as to neutralize all acids. It can destroy living organic matter as well as dead matter. A 1% solution of lye will kill lice, mites, and many kinds of bacteria, but is not strong enough to kill germs. When there is no disease in the bird rooms, this is the strength to be used inasmuch as it is not so harmful to the hands as a stronger solution. Whenever there is a serious contagious disease in the bird room, lye in 2% to 3% solution is essential to secure effective results. In using solutions of this strength the hands should be protected by rubbing vaseline into them before they are permitted to come in contact with the solution. Great care should be exercised to see that the solution does not get into the eyes. After the work is finished, the hands should be washed in warm water and rubbed with glycerin and olive oil in equal parts to prevent the chapping and cracking that always follows the withdrawal of oil from the skin. Lye does this, turning the oil in the skin into soap.

Most of the antiseptics in general use have the property of coagulating albumen. In such diseases as septic fever which are spread by means of scabs and viscid discharges that are composed largely of albumen, such disinfectants are of little value because by hardening the matter containing the germ they not only prevent their own access to them but also protect them from other agents that might kill them. This fact accounts for the great difficulty many breeders have experienced in attempting to stamp out septic fever once it has penetrated their bird rooms.

Sodium Acetate is the sodium salt of acetic acid. When you put baking soda in vinegar and drink it for a cold, you are taking a crude sodium acetate. It is a diuretic, aids in purifying the blood and may be useful in reducing over fat birds and bringing them into breeding condition. It is my opinion, however, that the citrates and tartarates are of more value. The chemical formula of pure sodium acetate is $NaC_2H_3O_2$ plus $3H_2O$.

Sodium Benzoate is the sodium salt of benzoic acid, $NaC_7H_5O_2$ plus H_2O. It appears on the market as a white powder, granulated or in the form of crystals, is soluble in 1:6 parts of water at room temperature. It is an antirheumatic, antiseptic, and antipyretic, used in rheumatism, gout, uremia, and fevers. This is the safest and best salt of this acid to use. For methods of using and dosage see **Benzoic Acid.**

Sodium Bicarbonate. This acid sodium salt of carbonic acid, $NaHCO_3$, is an antiacid because carbonic acid is so weak in acid properties that almost any other acid will decompose its salts with the liberation of carbon-dioxide gas. This fact is made use of in the preparation of all effervescent mixtures. Citric and tartaric acid are generally used for the reason that they are solids at room temperatures and that their sodium salts are very valuable therapeutic agents.

In addition to being an antiacid, sodium bicarbonate is also of some value as an antiseptic and antipyretic.

Sodium bicarbonate should not be given as an acid antidote in poisoning by acids, as the large amounts of carbon-dioxide given off are likely to rupture the stomach. Lime water or calcium or calcium carbonate are much preferable for this purpose.

Sodium Chloride is the sodium salt of hydrochloride acid, NaCl. The familiar, common table salt is almost pure sodium chloride and its uses have been discussed under Feeding.

Sodium Citrate. There are two sodium citrates: the neutral citrate and the acid citrate, both valuable as diuretics and antipyretics in the treatment of fevers. As a rule they are not used alone but are formed when effervescent salts containing citric acid and sodium bicarbonate are placed in water.

Sodium Fluoride, NaF, is the sodium salt of hydrofluoric acid, found on the market in the form of clear crystals or as a white powder. It is used internally as an antispasm in human medicine but is never used internally on birds.

Sodium fluoride is also a powerful antiseptic, disinfectant, and insecticide. I have mentioned its use as a treatment for lice in discussing those insects. A 25% powder will kill any insect with which it comes in contact, and in addition to being useful for treating bird-lice it is of value to dust into cracks and crevices to destroy mites and roaches.

Used in solution sodium fluoride will destroy all forms of bacteria and the eggs and nits of all insects. This makes it an excellent antiseptic wash for cages as well as a sterilizing liquid for instruments. It does not harm nickel-plating. A solution containing 0.75%, that is, one ounce to the gallon of sodium fluoride, is not very harmful to the hands and is a very powerful disinfectant, having the same property of dissolving oils and tissue as is possessed by sodium hydroxide. When used in solutions stronger than the one indicated, the hands should be protected just as for lye, and both substances should be kept out of the eyes. Although the 25% powder is not harmful to the eyes of a bird, it is rather painful for a few moments. When taken into the stomach in large quantities sodium fluoride is a poison; thus it is often used for poisoning mice by mixing it with one part sugar and two parts white flour and dusting on food that they like to eat. It is a rather slow-acting poison characterized in its action by severe cramps in the stomach. A mouse poisoned with sodium fluoride may be seen walking with the abdomen drawn in and the back humped up in an attitude of great pain for as long a period as twelve hours after eating the food. For that reason this method of killing mice should be avoided; traps are more humane. It is necessary to kill vermin, but needless cruelty even to those filthy creatures is inexcusable. Where sodium fluoride poisoning results from accident, the antidote is large quantities of olive oil and of water in which white of egg has been dissolved.

Sodium Iodide, NaI, is the sodium salt of hydroiodic acid. The physical properties, chemical reactions, medical uses, and dosages are the same as those of the potassium salt. The potassium salt is the one most used.

Sodium Phosphate, Dibasic, exsiccated. This comes commercially in the form of colorless crystals, containing water, as well as in the exsiccated form, which usually is sold as a white powder: its formula is Na_2HPO_4. It is a carthartic and is largely used in saline mixtures designed to have a purifying action on the liver. It is one of the constituents of my specific. I have cured birds suffering from septic fever with sodium phosphate and Potassium Permanganate, the latter used externally. The dose for a bird is one teaspoonful to the quart of drinking water.

Effervescent Sodium Phosphate contains the following:

      200 parts of exsiccated sodium phosphate
      477 parts of bicarbonate of soda
      252 parts of citric acid
      162 parts of tartaric acid

The citric acid and one-half of the sodium bicarbonate are first mixed and then dried in the air. To this the other ingredients are added and the mixture is stored in closed jars. The formula given is the official U.S.P. standard. The dose for a human being is one to four teaspoonsful in water; for a bird one teaspoonful to the quart of drinking water. This is a very good mixture, but for birds my own formula is preferable.

There are two other sodium phosphates: the monobasic and the tribasic. The former is used only in conjunction with Urotropin, as it has the power of making the blood and urine acid in reaction. The latter is not used in bird medicine. The monobasic salt is generally called *acid sodium phosphate*.

Sodium Salicylate, $NaC_7H_5O_2$, is the sodium salt of salicylic acid. This white powder is soluble in 0.9 parts of water at room temperature and is the best form in which to give salicylic acid. It is an antirheumatic, antiseptic, and antipyretic. For uses and dosage see the acid.

Sodium Silicate, a soluble glass made from sand and soda, is used in thick solution for setting limbs. It is impossible to put a splint on a bird's leg above the joint so that it will stay and the leg heal straight. It is a simple matter, however, to set such breaks in waterglass. The bird is wrapped in a bandage so that it cannot struggle and a few shreds of cotton are wrapped around the leg where it is broken. Then while the ends of the bones are held in place, the cotton is painted with the water-glass and permitted to set. If the job has been well done the leg will heal straight. After ten days the cast is soaked in warm water to which a very little lye has been added (0.5%) and the cotton cut away carefully. A splint may be used when the break is below the joint. A broken wing should never be set.[15] The bird should be placed in a cage having only low perches and left quietly for ten days. It is best to turn out the light while putting in food and water so that the bird will not try to use the wing. No examination should be made of the break for this is sure to irritate it. In nine cases out of ten the muscles of the broken wing will hold the limb in the correct position to permit the bone to heal straight. This will not be the case, however, if the bird is worried or excited.

Sodium Sulphate, Na_2SO_4 plus $10H_2O$, the sodium salt of sulphuric acid, is sold in the form of large colorless crystals, white granules, or a white powder. It can also be had free of water and then comes as a heavy white

---

[15] I have found it useful in such cases to tie the tips of the wings together very tightly over the tail with a fine thread, rosined or glued to make it hold. (Editor's Note.)

powder. This cathartic and diuretic has a bitter saline taste and is soluble in 2.8 parts of water at room temperature.

This is the well known *Glauber's Salt* so often recommended in the treatment of bird diseases. It is one of the best laxatives known for both birds and human beings, having the advantage of being less irritating than Epsom Salts, so much used in human medicine. Discussing this salt with a doctor once, he said, "Why is it that you insist on using Glauber's Salt on your birds? Veterinarians are the same way. I asked one once why he did not give Epsom Salts to a horse and he laughed at me. Why is it?"

"The best reason I know of," I replied, "is that a horse or bird is worth more than a man, and then, too, a man is the only animal that is fool enough to take anything you suggest to him."

And it is a fact that the popularity of this salt as a laxative is well justified, but its action is much improved by using it in effervescent mixtures.

Strychnine is a highly poisonous alkaloid from the seed of Nux Vomica. The formula is $C_{21}H_{22}N_2O_2$. Its only use in the bird room is as a tonic elixir and as a heart stimulant which has been discussed elsewhere.[16] The dose for a canary is from 1/7200 grain to 1/2400 grain to the ounce of drinking water. This amount is obtained by dissolving 1 grain in 60 fluid drams, or 7½ fluid ounces of whatever liquid medium is to be used. It is then given as a dose one to three drops to the ounce of drinking water; or a 1/60 grain tablet can be dissolved in one teaspoonful of water and one to three drops of this given in the drinking water. The dose of three drops to the

---

[16] Elixir of Iron, Quinine, and Strychnine Phosphates, page 204; Iron, Quinine and Strychnine Citrate, page 206.

ounce of drinking water is the one to be used where a powerful heart stimulant is needed, but this should not be used for two days in succession.

Syrup of Hypophosphites contains Calcium Hypophosphite, 4.5%; Potassium Hypophosphite, 1.5%; Sodium Hypophosphite, 1.5%; dilute Hypophosphorous acid, 0.2%; sugar, 65%; tincture of fresh lemon peel, 0.5%; and water to make up to 100%.

Compound Syrup of Hypophosphites contains Calcium Hypophosphite, 3.5%; Potassium Hypophosphite, 1.75%; Sodium Hypophosphite, 1.75%; Ferric Hypophosphite, 0.225%; Manganese Hypophosphite, 0.225%; Quinine, 0.11%; Strychnine, 0.0115%; Sodium Citrate, 0.375%; Dilute Hypophosphorous Acid, 1.5%; Sugar, 77.5%; and water to make up 100%.

Both of these are standard U.S.P. preparations and may be had at any drug store. They are used as tonics for birds in a run-down condition and are usually given with cod liver oil. The second prescription is the better of the two for it contains iron, quinine, and strychnine in addition to the other hypophosphites. The dose for a bird is two to six drops to the ounce of drinking water.

Taraxacum Juice is the juice pressed from fresh dandelion roots that have been gathered in the fall of the year and preserved in alcohol. It contains taraxacin, taraxacerin, resin, levulin, inulin, and pectin. It is especially good as a tonic in liver and splenic enlargement. The dose for a bird is from 3 to 10 drops to the ounce of drinking water.

The tonic properties of the dandelion are well known to bird breeders and canaries and many wild birds eat this plant with relish. It is the one plant of which the canary will eat every part except the petals. It should be fed fresh as often as possible; when this is done, there will be fewer calls for the bird doctor.

RULES FOR DOSES

All standard works on drugs refer only to their use on human subjects, and in order to make the information contained in them available as a basis upon which to rest the experimental treatment of birds some method of converting human dosages into bird dosages must be available. From my own experiments I have worked out the following rules:

For saline laxatives and diuretics where the human dose is from one to four drams (a dram is a level teaspoonful), the dose for a bird is the minimum human dose added to one quart of drinking water.

For tonics where the human dose is one teaspoonful three times per day, the bird dose is one to three drops to the ounce of drinking water. Where these tonics contain powerful stimulants such as strychnine, digitalis, etc., the time that it takes a bird to reach the limit of tolerance is about half the time that it takes a human being to reach that condition.

In powerful drugs, and especially the alkaloids, where the human dose is figured in grains or fractions of grains three times per day, the dose for a bird will be from 1/200 to 1/100 of the single human dose. Such drugs are diluted with sugar as explained elsewhere. The minimum human dose is mixed with **100 parts of sugar** and then a quantity of this mixture equal by weight to ½ to 1½ times the weight of the human dose is sprinkled on a small amount of soft food. It must be remembered that in giving drugs by this method the bird gets the entire amount used if the amount of food taken is such that the bird will eat it all, while diluting drugs in the drinking water the bird gets only about 1/10 the amount of the drug used if the water is left before it for twelve hours.

In following these rules it will soon be noted that there are many exceptions. Birds are much less sensitive to some drugs than are mammals, and to some others they are much more sensitive than mammals. For that reason it is always best to start with the minimum dose indicated by the rules just given and then increase the dosage until expected therapeutic reaction takes place or ill effects are noted. In many cases it is necessary to give the medicine by means of a dropper since some birds will not drink at all or drink only a little of the medicated liquid.

Whenever giving a treatment for anything except a contagious disease (in that case you follow the directions as given for that disease), as soon as you note improvement give the treatment in grodually diminishing quantities or discontinue it for a day. Then if the bird seems worse again the treatment may be repeated. It is much better to go slowly than to overdose.

DISEASES OF CANARIES
INDEX

A

Acetic Acid 180
Air Sacs 23
Aluminum and Potassium Sulphate 186
Ammoniac 186
Ammonium Benzoate 187
Antiseptic for hands (Creolin) 196
Antiseptic, intestinal (Creosote) 196
Antiseptic for lungs and kidneys (Benzoic Acid)............180
Antiseptic, mild (Boric Acid) 181
Apoplectiform Septicemia 113
Apoplectiform Septicemia, streptococcus of 114, 163
Appetite, lack of...141
Argyrol, method of using..219
Arteries 12
Aspergillosis 139
Aspergillus Fumigatus 139
Aspergillus infection (Potassium Iodide) 215
Asthma 141
    (Ammonium) Benzoate 187

B

Bacillery White Diarrhoea 131
Bacillus Canariensis Necrophorus 170
Bacillus Coli 176
Bacteriology 152
B. Paratyphosus B 105, 108, 166
B. Paratyphosus B. infection (Iron Sulphate)................203
Bacterium Pullorum 132, 135
B. Sanguinarium 135
Baldness 78
    Congenital 81
    Due to destruction of feathers............................... 83
    Due to exhaustion 83
    Due to lack of necessary food............................... 83
    Due to upset moult 82
    Kinds of 81
    Treatment of 84
Benzoic Acid 180
Bird Pox 103
Birds in Flight Cages 54
Bismuth 188
    Citrate 188
    Lactate 188
    Subgallate 188
    Subnitrate 189
Bleeding, stop (Aluminum and Potassium Sulphate).....186
    (Copper Sulphate) 195
    (Iron Chloride) 202
Blister 100
Blisters, water 110

INDEX

Blood	12
Blood Cultures	159
Boric Acid	181
Bowels, Chronic inflammation of (Salicylic Acid)	184
Brain	15
Bread	59
Breathing, increased rate of	100, 105, 111, 136
Breathing, rapid	141
Breeding Birds	54
Breeding Condition, getting birds into (Citric Acid)	182
(Iron and Quinine Citrate—Green)	205
Breeding exhaustion from	35
Broken Bones	89
Brooder Pneumonia	139

C

Cages, wash (Carbolic Acid)	181
(Creolin)	196
Calcium	190
Calcium Glycerinophosphate	190
Calcium Permanganate	191
Calcium Peroxide	191
Calcium Sachharate	192
Calcium Tribiasic Phosphate	192
Camphor Gum	192
Canary Necrosis	103
(Iron Sulphate)	203
Canary Seed	52
Cancer	142
Carbolic Acid	181
Cascara Sagrada	193
Castor Oil	212
Cathartic (Castor Oil)	212
(Sodium Phosphate)	224
Catarrh, chronic (Ammoniac)	186
Chicks, dead in the shell	37, 48
Chicks, dying	131
Chinosol	142
Cholera, hog	166
Chrysanthemum Flowers	194
Cinchona	194
Circulatory System	10
Citric Acid	182
Citrocarbonate	183
Cleaning Glass (Oxalic Acid)	183
Cleansing Agent (Sodium Hydroxide)	220
Clear Eggs	38, 47
Cod Liver Oil	212
Colds (Ammoniac)	186
(Benzoic Acid)	180
(Cinchona)	194
(Glycerin)	198
(Naphthalene)	208

DISEASES OF CANARIES

```
(Silver Protein Preparations) .................................................. 218
Color Food .................................................................................. 63
    (Geranium) ...................................................................... 198
    (Nasturtium) .................................................................. 211
Contagious Diseases (Hydrogen Peroxide) ...................... 200
Copper Sulphate ................................................................ 195
Creolin ................................................................................ 196
Creosote ............................................................................. 196
Crop ..................................................................................... 18
Cultures, Taking ............................................................... 155
```

D

```
Diagnosis, introduction to ............................................... 146
Diarrhoea ........................................................................... 141
    (Bismuth Lactate) ........................................................ 188
    (Bismuth Subgallate) .................................................. 188
    (Naphthalene) .............................................................. 208
    Bacillery white ............................................................. 131
    Green or bloody .................................................. 106, 111
    Nestling ......................................................................... 128
    Soft, whitish, pasty .................................................... 132
Digestive Disorder ............................................................. 44
Digestive Tract ................................................................... 16
Diphtheria, avian ............................................................. 103
Doses, Rules for ............................................................... 228
Droppings, color of .......................................................... 100
    Dirty cream .................................................................. 129
    Greenish ........................................................................ 115
    Thick, white and chalky ............................................ 136
    Watery ........................................................................... 136
    Yellow .................................................................. 105, 111
    Yellow ........................................................................... 125
```

E

```
Egg Food .............................................................................. 55
    Rupture ........................................................................... 95
    Yolk, dried ...................................................................... 60
    Clear ......................................................................... 37, 47
```

F

```
Feather Mite ........................................................................ 70
Feathers ............................................................................... 26
    Fluffed ............................................................ 107, 115, 136
    Ingrown (Silver Nitrate) ............................................ 218
Feet, dirty ............................................................................ 69
    Swollen ......................................................................... 133
Fits ..................................................................................... 115
Food, refuses .................................................................... 119
Foot, lame ......................................................................... 107
Formula No. 1 ..................................................................... 58
Formula No. 2 ..................................................................... 58
```

INDEX 233

Formula No. 3 59
Formula No. 4 60
Fowl Cholera 119, 124, 126
    Germ of 162
Fowl Typhoid 165
Fractured Legs (Sodium Silicate) 225
Freese Disease 171
Friar's Balsam (Benzoic Acid) 180
Fungoid skin (Acetic Acid) 180

G

Gape 71
General Management 55
Gentian 197
Geranium 198
Gizzard 19
Glauber's Salts 226
Glycerin 198
Glycerite, Iron, Quinine, and Strychnine Phosphates 199
Glycyrrhiza 199
Glycyrrhizin Ammoniate 199
Going Light 41, 142
Green Food 35, 53

H

Heart 10
    Hemorrhages in 125
    Stimulant (Strychnine) 226
Hemorrhagic Septicemia 103, 122
Hemp Seed 29, 52
Hexamethylenamine 199
Hydrogen Peroxide 200
Hyphophosphites, Syrup of 39, 227
Hypophosphites, Compound Syrup of 227

I

Incubation, Period of 27
Indigestion (Calcium Sachharate) 192
    (Salicylic Acid) 184
    Due to improper feeding during moult 76
    Following moult 39, 40
Infections, local skin (Tincture of Iodine) 202
Infectious Necrosis, organism of 170
Injuries and Accidents 89
Insecticide (Creolin) 196
Insects as food 62
Intestines 19
Intestines, inflamed 137
    Red and Swollen 172
Iodine 201
    Source of assimilable (Potassium Iodide) 215

DISEASES OF CANARIES

Iodides 37
Iron 41, 202
    Acetate 202
    Ammonium Citrate 203
    Chloride 202
    Citrate 203
    Effervescent Citrate of 203
    And Quinine Citrate—Brown 205
    And Quinine Citrate—Green 205
    Quinine and Strychnine Citrate 206
    Quinine, and Strychnine Phosphate, Elixir of 204
    I. Q. S. tonic 41
    Citro-Iodine, Syrup of 203
    Sulphate 203

J

Jesuit's Drops (Benzoic Acid) 180

K

Kidneys, enlarged 137

L

Lameness 144
Laxative (Olive Oil) 213
    (Sodium Sulphate) 225
Leg 8
Leg, broken 92
Lice (Chrysanthemum) 194
    (Lysol) 208
    (Naphthalene) 208
    (Sodium Fluoride) 222
Lice and Mites 67
Lime 207
Liver 20
    Enlarged 136, 172, 174
    Mulberry 126
    Yellow 172
    Yellow bands on 137
    Yellow nodules in 120
Loss of weight 44
Lumps (Silver Nitrate) 218
Lungs 23
Lye 220
Lymphatic System 14
Lysol 208

M

Male, singing 53
Maw Seed (Opium) 213

INDEX

Meat	58
Milk	31
Mineral Food	53
Mineral Food Formulae	63
Minerals	35
Mites	68
(Camphor Gum)	192
(Chrysanthemum)	194
(Lysol)	208
Mosquito bites, treatment of	67
Mosquitoes	66
Mothers not feeding	129, 131
Moult	79
Controlled by drugs	75
Controlled by temperature	75
Exhaustion from	35
Physiology of	74
Stuck in	76
Moulting of breeding stock	86
Mouth	16
Muscles	9
Mycosis	142

N

Naphthalene	208
Nasturtium	211
Necrosis, infectious	119
Nervous system	15
Nervous twitchings	44
Nest, damp and foul	129
Delousing (Naphthalene)	208
Keeping mites out of	68
Nestling diarrhoea	128
Nostrils	21
Nux Vomica	212

O

Oidium Albicans	131
Olive Oil	213
Opium	213
Orange Oil	213
Overfat birds (Citric Acid)	182
(Citrocarbonate)	183
Overfeeding (Sulphuric Acid)	185
Liver trouble due to (Acetic Acid)	180
Oxalic Acid	183
Antidote for	184

P

Paralyzed	116
Pasteurella Avian	105, 124, 162
Pathology	148

DISEASES OF CANARIES

Pelvis	8
Phosphates	38
Pneumococcus	105
Potassium Chlorate	214
Iodide	215
Permanganate	216
Potato, Cold Boiled	59
Pratt's Buttermilk Baby-Chick Food	60
Proventriculus	18
Psittacosis	108, 110
Puffed abdomen	108
Puffed up	124
Pullorum, Bacterium	132
Pulse	28
Pyrethrum	69, 194

Q

Quassia	217
Quinine	217

R

Rape Seed	51
German summer	51
Rubson	51
Ribs	6
Rickets	46, 47
Respiration	28
Organs of	21
Reproductive Organs—Female	24
Male	24
Reproductive Vitamine	49

S

Salicylic Acid	184
Salt	35
Poisonous effects of	36
Sanguinarium Bacterium	165
Scaly-Leg (Carbolic Acid)	181
(Glycerin)	198
Scaly-Leg Mite	69
Seed, mouldy	145
Seeds, storing of (Naphthalene)	208
Septicemic diseases (Copper Sulphate)	195
Septic Fever	97
(Citric Acid)	182
(Iron Sulphate)	203
(Potassium Chlorate)	214
(Sodium Phosphate)	224
Shivering	115
Silicon	40
Silver Nitrate	218

INDEX

Silver Protein Preparations	218
Skeleton	3, 5
Skin	25
Infections (Citric Acid)	182
Skull	3
Sleeps a great deal	124
Most of time	136
Slipped Claw	94
Sodium	219
Acetate	221
Benzoate	221
Bicarbonate	221
Citrate	222
Chloride	222
Fluoride	222
Hydroxide	220
Iodide	223
Phosphate	224
Salicylate	224
Silicate	225
Sulphate	225
Soft Moult	32, 75
(Citrocarbonate)	183
(Iron Ammonium Citrate)	203
(Iron and Quinine Citrate—Green)	205
(I.Q.S. Phosphates, Elixir of)	204
Song restorers	63
Sores on feet	66
Treating (Potassium Permanganate)	216
Specimens, Taking	152
Spinal Cord	15
Spleen	21
Enlarged	119, 137
Splint (Sodium Silicate)	225
Sporadic Pneumonia, Organisms of	173
Staphlococcus Pyogenus Aureus	174
Starvation, run-down condition from (Calcium Glycerinophosphate)	190
Sterilizer (Tincture of Iodine)	202
Sternum	6
Stomach disorders (Ammonium Benzoate)	187
Stimulant (Bismuth Citrate)	188
Streptococcus pyogenus	105, 110
Strychnine	226
Suisepticum, Bacterium	165
Sulphur	39
Sulphuric Acid	185
Swallow, trying to	71
Sweating hens	129
Symptoms, observation of	146

T

Taraxacum Juice	227
Tartaric Acid	185

Temperature, normal 27
Thrush 131
    (Potassium Iodide) 215
Thyroid extract 75
    Residue 76
Tincture of Iodine 202
Toes Swollen 66
Tongue, dry and hard (Glycerin) 198
Tonic **(Cascara)** 193
    (Cinchona) 194
    (Creosote) 196
    (Effervescent Citrate of Iron) 203
    (Gentian) 197
    (Iron Acetate) 202
    (Iron Citro-Iodine, Syrup of) 203
    (Iron Chloride) 202
    (I.Q.S. Citrate) 206
    (I.Q.S. Phosphates, Elixir of) 204
    (Iron and Quinine Citrate—Green) 205
    (Hypophosphites, Compound Syrup of) 227
    (Nux Vomica) 212
    (Quassia) 217
    (Sulphuric Acid) 135
    (Taraxacum Juice) 227
    Nerve (Calcium Glycerinophosphate) 190
Tonic Seed 53, 63
Turkington's Balsam (Benzoic Acid) 180

U

Urinary System 23
Uterus, prolapse of the 96

V

Veins 12
Vent, inflamed 95
Vertebral Column 4
Viscera 17
Vitamine A 43
    B 44
    C 45
    D 46
    D, methods of supplying 48
Vitamines 42
Vitaminosis 42
    A 43
    B 44
    D 47
Voice, change of 105

INDEX

W

Waterberry's Tonic (Creosote) ...196
Weakness ...141
White-wash (Lime) ...207
Wing ...7
    Broken ...89
    Drooped ...145
    Growth in ...145
    Lame ...107
Worms (Creosote) ...196
    (Naphthalene) ...208
    In windpipe ...71
    Removal of intestinal (Calcium Sachharate) ...192
Wound dressing (Boric Acid) ...181